PALATE *cleanser*

HILTON HEAD ISLAND
SOUTH CAROLINA

Find your way to America's Favorite Island®.
32.2163° N, 80.7526° W

HiltonHeadIsland.org

SAVANNAH HILTON HEAD INTERNATIONAL

WINNER TRAVEL+LEISURE WORLD'S BEST AWARDS 2021

South Carolina Just right.

What does fiduciary mean to you?

Justina L.
Independent financial advisor since 2015

It's more than acting in the best interest of my clients. It's being responsible. Proactive. Involved in every aspect of their financial well-being.

FindYourIndependentAdvisor.com

Scan now to find a local advisor.

charles SCHWAB

Own your tomorrow.

"**Every day is full of inspiration and I try to give back to the city the same passion it gives me.**"

José Andrés with his relief efforts provided through World Central Kitchen; the Trois Mec kitchen produced 300 to 400 meals a day. As a Lexus Culinary Master, I was also able to partner with them during the pandemic. Lexus provided funds for a grocery program for our employees. We also worked together on a program to deliver Valentine's Day meals. It was really nice knowing that we were able to impact people's lives with a simple meal.

Tell us how it was to be a featured Lexus Culinary Master at this year's *Food & Wine* Classic in Aspen?

Lexus is such an amazing supporter of the culinary arts. It was an honor to be selected as a Lexus Culinary Master back in 2018. And I love being a part of these events because they allow us, as chefs, to get together and brainstorm ideas, share stories, and have real life contact with a support system. It's also so nice to be with festival attendees—one of the

hardest things for me during the pandemic was not having that one-on-one contact with my guests.

So, what is exciting you about cooking these days?

During the pandemic I opened a wood fire grill kebab pop-up, called Ludobab. I am excited about continuing to see this grow. And I am really excited about opening my first restaurant outside of L.A., in Denver this fall/winter. We have named the restaurant, Chez Maggy, in honor of my

late mother-in-law, and the menu will be an "All France" brasserie. It is an incredibly personal project, as Denver has always been a second home to my family—and to be able to honor my mother-in-law and her impact on our lives makes this so much more than a restaurant opening.

Stephanie Izard

Master of **Her Craft**

Lexus Culinary Master Chef Stephanie Izard talks about her move out west, the lessons of the last year, and her undying love of "all things crunchy."

CHICAGO'S CULINARY SCENE has been booming these last few years—and a large part of that is thanks to Stephanie Izard. The first-ever woman to win "Top Chef" (she earned that title back in 2008), as well as a James Bead Award winner, designated Iron Chef, and Lexus Culinary Master, Izard has created an ever-growing empire in the city in which she was born. "Not only does Chicago have an amazing energy, but the chef community is really tight knit," she notes.

When Izard opened the now-iconic Girl & the Goat in the West Loop some 11 years ago, "it was wildly different than it is now," she says, "so it's been exciting to see the

neighborhood evolve, and to grow along with it." Izard's growth has involved opening other restaurant concepts in the area, including the diner-style Little Goat, the Chinese-flavored Duck Duck Goat, the Peruvian-influenced Cabra, and the Sugargoat bakery. She also has a line of cooking sauces and spices, a nationwide meal kit service, and is the author of two cookbooks.

We caught up with the visionary chef just after the opening of her first restaurant outside of Chicago—an L.A. outpost of Girl & the Goat—to talk about her new venture, her current inspirations, and her love of mentoring emerging talent.

"It's been really rewarding to mentor and foster talent in chefs."

are always a lot of fun—I love connecting with guests—and this year my demo featured ingredients from my retail line.

But Lexus is also an amazing partner. They helped fund meals and stipends for our staff who were out of work during the pandemic, and they were a major sponsor of a philanthropic event I helped host for Equality Should Be Normal, a local Chicago organization whose mission is to eradicate racism.

We know you just opened a new restaurant—but any other plans in the works for the future?

I've always seen myself as a hardworking chef, right in the thick of it next to my team. It's been really rewarding to mentor and foster talent in chefs, and I'd like to continue helping the next generation take the leap to find their own paths.

Otherwise, I've been focused on my never-ending search for all things crunchy! Not only did This Little Goat launch our "Everything Crunch" line of toppings, but our team has been playing with textures at Girl & the Goat. And, now that the world is opening back up, I'm excited to start traveling again and experiencing new cuisines and cultures.

Q+A

Following all your success in Chicago, what made you head to Los Angeles?

Besides the obvious incredible weather, L.A.'s Art District reminds me a lot of Chicago's West Loop a few years ago. It has so much soul and creativity. We've kept a few of the Girl & the Goat classics on the menu, but we're also excited to play with new, local ingredients – I've been taking a lot of trips to the Farmer's Market.

Back in Chicago, have you made changes at your restaurants following the lockdowns?

The pandemic allowed restaurateurs to take a step back and reevaluate how we work. It forced us to get creative, connect with guests on another level, and really let our compassion shine. That also applies to our internal team. We want to make sure that we have a safe and fun work environment, where staff feels heard, respected, and challenged.

What has the experience been like being a Lexus Culinary Master?

I became a Lexus Culinary Master in 2014, and I've loved being part of all the fun event opportunities with the brand, such as the *Food & Wine* Classic in Aspen. Cooking demos

Tiffany Pham
CEO of Mogul & Speaker
Supports diverse individuals to unlock
their potential and reach success.

CLASSIC
FOOD&WINE
MEMBER

Acclaimed for exquisite design, advanced technology, and the cooking performance required of a Food & Wine Classic in Aspen Official Partner, Monogram is redefining luxury one detail at a time.

Discover the appliances featured at the iconic event at monogram.com

MONOGRAM™
LUXURY APPLIANCES

05

the world
is reopening
Open up to
the World

GOLDEN KNIGHTS & POCKET KINGS

The best of Vegas excitement is at ARIA.
With the five-star award-winning Sky Suites and the pinnacle
in entertainment a few steps away at Park Theater and
T-Mobile® Arena. A dining destination that exceeds with
highly sought-after culinary experiences like Carbone,
Catch, Din Tai Fung and more. Add unmatched service,
private poolside cabanas and rejuvenating spa
treatments to a full itinerary that can't be missed.

BOOK NOW AT ARIA.COM

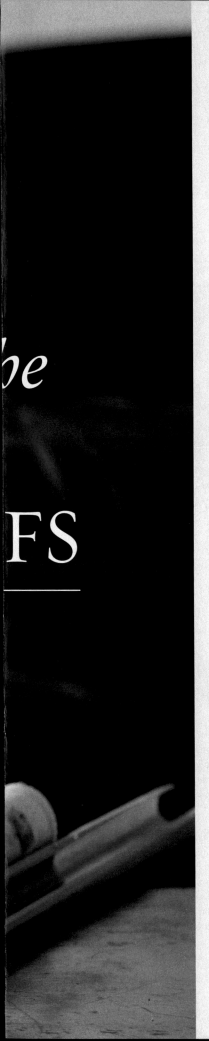

EFFORTLESSLY COOL KITCHEN DESIGN

Discover a perfect harmony of form and function with the beautifully designed, 36-inch Monolith French door refrigerator with bottom freezer.

REDEFINE YOUR SPACE

A refrigerator is the largest appliance in your kitchen and a new one is a simple way to refresh or update the aesthetic of this much-loved room. With this latest addition to the Monolith Collection by Liebherr, elegant French doors (which open out silently and independently of each other) create extra space and easy access when you're grabbing a snack or selecting ingredients for a recipe. Inside, a seamlessly integrated InfinityLight LED lighting system beautifully illuminates the entire space so you can find what you need in a snap.

KEEP FOOD FRESHER WITH BIOFRESH

High-quality refrigeration preserves the flavor and integrity of your ingredients, from fruits and veggies to fine cuts of meat and succulent seafood. To keep food in peak condition, the whisper-quiet PowerCooling system maintains an even temperature throughout, including circulating cold air through the door. For added precision, BioFresh-Plus technology allows you to compartmentalize for different products, such as keeping dairy well-chilled and fish in market-like conditions.

UPGRADE WITH SMART FEATURES

Thanks to the intuitive InfinitySwipe, touch-control panel, adjusting your Monolith refrigerator is simple. To change the temperature or other settings, touch and swipe through a full-color, user-friendly 3.5-inch display. You can also control your refrigerator right from your smartphone or tablet with the SmartDeviceBox, which allows you to activate settings and features when you're on the go.

Explore the Monolith Collection at **home.liebherr.com/monolith**.

UNRIVALED
SPACE AT SEA™

The luxury of personal space is central to the promise of An Unrivaled Experience®
with Regent Seven Seas Cruises®. It provides the extravagant freedom guests need to
explore and relax to the fullest. As the preeminent luxury cruise line on the ocean, we pride
ourselves in offering some of the largest balconies and most spacious suites at sea. Our wide
range of specialty restaurants, al fresco and in-suite dining options, exquisite lounges, bars
and expansive spaces are perfect to rest and celebrate in, knowing there is never a queue
or a crowd and that every detail is taken care of and every amenity is included.

Join us and discover how — with our unrivaled space at sea — we will exceed
your loftiest expectations of comfort and personalized service for a truly
unforgettable experience aboard The World's Most Luxurious Fleet™.

START YOUR JOURNEY AT RSSC.COM
CALL **1.844.473.4368** OR CONTACT YOUR TRAVEL ADVISOR

Regent
SEVEN SEAS CRUISES®

AN UNRIVALED EXPERIENCE®

For the latest details on our health and safety protocols, please visit **RSSC.com/HealthSafetyProtocols**

EVERY
LUXURY
INCLUDED

*The Table Salad
from Saint-Germain
in New Orleans
(see story p. 156)*

The Restaurant Issue

ON THE COVER *photography by* AUBRIE PICK

74

STAFF-FAVORITE
PAIRING

**CHARRED
CAULIFLOWER
TACOS WITH
ROMESCO SALSA**
with Mexican
pilsner: Modelo
Especial

90

STAFF-FAVORITE
PAIRING

**SKIRT STEAKS
WITH CARROT
PUREE AND
BRAISED
CABBAGE**
*with ripe, low-
tannin red: 2018
St. Francis Old
Vines Zinfandel*

COOK
THE
COVER

FOR THE COVER RECIPE, SWEET POTATO STICKY BUNS WITH TOASTED MARSHMALLOW FROM
L.A.'S ALL DAY BABY, SEE FOODANDWINE.COM/SWEET-POTATO-STICKY-BUNS.

What Ray's Pouring Now Executive Wine Editor
Ray Isle's favorite things to drink this month

**2020 FRITZ HAAG ESTATE
RIESLING TROCKEN** *($20)*

*Weingut Fritz Haag is one of the
undisputed stars of Germany's Mosel
River valley, and what a super deal
this crystalline-minerally, dry Riesling
is! It's one to buy by the case and
serve all autumn long—possibly with
pork tenderloin roasted with apples.*

2019 REVELSHINE RED *($15)*

*This light-bodied, freshly fruity
blend, which Limerick Lane winemaker Jake Bilbro makes from
organically farmed grapes, comes in
an unbreakable, recyclable alumi-
num can. It's a great choice for
camping trips, beach cookouts, and
lowering your carbon footprint, too.*

**2015 SEI QUERCE RANCH
HOUSE CABERNET SAUVIGNON**
($79)

*Sei Querce is another winery working
to offset its carbon emissions. I had
this Sonoma Cabernet on a cool night
in Maine, and its rich, dark-berried
fruit and supple tannins were stellar
with a rib eye straight off the grill.*

Food & Wine (ISSN 0741-9015) (October 2021) (Volume 44/Issue 10) is published monthly by TI Inc. Affluent Media Group, a subsidiary of Meredith Corporation. Principal Office: 225 Liberty St., New York, NY 10281-1008. Periodicals postage paid at New York, NY, and additional mailing offices. Postmaster: Send all UAA to CFS. (See DMM 507.1.5.2) Non-Postal and Military Facilities: Send address corrections to Food & Wine Magazine, PO Box 37508 Boone, IA 50037-0508. Canada Post Publications Mail Agreement # 40069223. BN# 12948036 4RT. © All Rights Reserved. Printed in the U.S.A. Customer Service and Subscriptions: For 24/7 service, please use our website: foodandwine.com/myaccount. You can also call 1-800-333-6569 or write Food & Wine, PO Box 37508 Boone, IA 50037-0508. Reproduction in whole or in part without written permission is strictly prohibited. Your bank may provide updates to the card information we have on file. You may opt out of this service at any time. Member of the Alliance for Audited Media.

ILLUSTRATION: RACHEL CARNEY

Alliance for
Audited Media

Chief financial officer. Caregiver. Eclipse chaser.
A life well planned allows you to

LIVE *YOUR* LIFE.

——

While you may not be closing a business deal and taking your mother and daughter on a once-in-a-lifetime adventure — your life is just as unique. Backed by sophisticated resources and a team of specialists in every field, a Raymond James financial advisor can help you plan for the dreams you have, the way you care for those you love and how you choose to give back. So you can live *your* life.

RAYMOND JAMES
LIFE WELL PLANNED.

FOOD&WINE

EDITOR IN CHIEF
Hunter Lewis

SENIOR DIRECTOR, CONTENT STRATEGY Michelle Edelbaum
DEPUTY EDITOR Melanie Hansche
EXECUTIVE EDITOR Karen Shimizu
EXECUTIVE WINE EDITOR Ray Isle
MANAGING EDITOR Caitlin Murphree Miller

FOOD & EDITORIAL

RESTAURANT EDITOR Khushbu Shah
SENIOR FOOD EDITOR Mary-Frances Heck
FOOD EDITOR Josh Miller
ASSOCIATE FOOD EDITOR Kelsey Youngman
ASSOCIATE CULTURE EDITOR Oset Babür-Winter
ASSOCIATE FEATURES EDITOR Nina Friend
BUSINESS MANAGER Alice Eldridge Summerville
EDITORIAL FELLOW Lauren Musni

COPY & RESEARCH

COPY EDITOR Erin Clyburn
COPY EDITOR Winn Duvall

ART

CREATIVE DIRECTOR Winslow Taft
ASSOCIATE ART DIRECTOR Khoa Tran
DESIGNER Rachel Carney

PHOTO

PHOTO DIRECTOR Tori Katherman
PHOTO EDITOR Dan Bailey

PRODUCTION

PRODUCTION DIRECTOR Liz Rhoades

DIGITAL

SENIOR EDITOR Kat Kinsman
SENIOR EDITOR Maria Yagoda
SENIOR SOCIAL MEDIA EDITOR Sam Gutierrez
ASSOCIATE NEWS EDITOR Adam Campbell-Schmitt
STAFF WRITER Bridget Hallinan
VISUALS EDITOR Sarah Crowder
DIGITAL OPERATIONS EDITOR Elsa Säätelä
E-COMMERCE EDITOR Megan Soll

CULINARY DIRECTOR AT LARGE Justin Chapple
EXECUTIVE PRODUCER Kwame Onwuachi

CONTRIBUTORS

Betsy Andrews, Steven Blaski, Beth Brinsfield,
Kate Cunningham, Charlotte Druckman,
Anthony Giglio, Joe Harper, Kate Heddings,
Megan Krigbaum, David Landsel, Clarissa León,
Andrea Nguyen, CB Owens, Jamila Robinson,
Gail Simmons, Joshua David Stein,
Julia Turshen, Andrew Zimmern

F&W COOKS

Jocelyn Delk Adams, Zoe Adjonyoh, Javier Cabral,
Samantha Fore, Paola Briseño González,
Leah Koenig, The League of Kitchens, Vallery Lomas,
David McCann, Hetty McKinnon, Andrea Nguyen,
Ann Taylor Pittman, Todd Richards,
Yasmin Sabir, Samantha Seneviratne, Nik Sharma,
Andrea Slonecker, Susan Spungen, Molly Stevens,
Pierre Thiam, Marcela Valladolid,
Hetal Vasavada, Karla T. Vasquez

VICE PRESIDENT/PUBLISHER
Tom Bair

ASSOCIATE PUBLISHER, MARKETING Kerri Fallon Dilley
EXECUTIVE DIRECTOR, GLOBAL SALES Vince Kooch

BRAND SALES

NEW YORK Caroline Donohue, R.W. Horton
CHICAGO Hillary Pavia
LOS ANGELES Lewis Newmark
MIAMI (BLUE GROUP MEDIA) Jill Stone, Eric Davis
NORTHWEST (SD MEDIA) Steve Dveris, Kelly Wagner
LAS VEGAS/SOUTHWEST/NORTHWEST (BAAK MEDIA) Tricia Baak
SOUTHWEST Jennifer Fan
BOSTON (WNP MEDIA) Jennifer Palmer
HAWAII (MEDIA LINKS) Laurie Doerschlen
ASIA Scott Thoreau
CANADA (DODD MEDIA) Bob Dodd, Lori Dodd
MEXICO (ADVANTAGE MEDIA) Pablo Glogovsky
SWITZERLAND (MEDIA INTERLINK SA) Neil Sartori
DIRECT MEDIA Breana Tolla
ADVERTISING COORDINATOR Paul Dispenza
ASSISTANTS Maria Garza, Alexandra Scelzo, Riley Shea, Tara Stacy

MARKETING

EXECUTIVE MARKETING DIRECTOR Amanda LaFontaine
DIRECTORS, BRAND MARKETING Antonia LoPresti Giglio, Kristi Naeris
BRAND STRATEGY DIRECTOR Cara Wolf Erwin
ASSOCIATE DIRECTOR, BRAND MARKETING Rob Sampogna
SENIOR MANAGER, BRAND MARKETING Doug Murphy
MANAGER, BRAND MARKETING Michelle Pallotta-Calcagni
EXECUTIVE DIRECTOR, EVENT MARKETING Diella Allen
ASSOCIATE DIRECTOR, EVENT MARKETING Amanda DeRienzo
EVENT MARKETING ASSOCIATE MANAGER Alexandra Perry
EVENT MARKETING COORDINATOR Hannah Soltys
MARKETING ASSISTANT Catherine Weppler
SPECIAL PROJECTS PRODUCER Devin Padgett

COMMUNICATIONS

SENIOR DIRECTOR, CORPORATE AND BRAND COMMUNICATIONS Elizabeth Marsh

OPERATIONS

PRODUCTION DIRECTOR Melanie Stoltenberg
PRODUCTION MANAGER April Gross
DIRECTOR OF QUALITY Joseph Kohler

HUMAN RESOURCES

DIRECTOR Carole Cain

MEREDITH NATIONAL MEDIA GROUP

PRESIDENT Catherine Levene
PRESIDENT, MEREDITH MAGAZINES Doug Olson
PRESIDENT, CONSUMER PRODUCTS Tom Witschi
PRESIDENT, MEREDITH DIGITAL Alysia Borsa
EVP, STRATEGIC & BUSINESS DEVELOPMENT Daphne Kwon

EXECUTIVE VICE PRESIDENTS

CHIEF REVENUE OFFICER Michael Brownstein
DIGITAL SALES Marla Newman
FINANCE Michael Riggs
MARKETING & INTEGRATED COMMUNICATIONS Nancy Weber

SENIOR VICE PRESIDENTS

GROUP PUBLISHER, LUXURY Giulio Capua
CONSUMER MARKETING Steve Crowe
CONSUMER REVENUE Andy Wilson
CORPORATE SALES Brian Kightlinger
FOUNDRY 360 Matt Petersen
PRODUCT & TECHNOLOGY Justin Law
RESEARCH SOLUTIONS Britta Cleveland
STRATEGIC PLANNING Amy Thind
STRATEGIC SOURCING, NEWSSTAND, PRODUCTION Chuck Howell

VICE PRESIDENTS

BRAND LICENSING Toye Cody, Sondra Newkirk
BUSINESS PLANNING & ANALYSIS Rob Silverstone
FINANCE Chris Susil
STRATEGIC DEVELOPMENT Kelsey Andersen
STRATEGIC PARTNERSHIPS Alicia Cervini
VICE PRESIDENT, GROUP EDITORIAL DIRECTOR Stephen Orr
CHIEF DIGITAL CONTENT OFFICER Amanda Dameron
DIRECTOR, EDITORIAL OPERATIONS & FINANCE Greg Kayko

MEREDITH CORPORATION

CHAIRMAN & CHIEF EXECUTIVE OFFICER Tom Harty
CHIEF FINANCIAL OFFICER Jason Frierott
CHIEF DEVELOPMENT OFFICER John Zieser
PRESIDENT, MEREDITH LOCAL MEDIA GROUP Patrick McCreery
SENIOR VICE PRESIDENT, HUMAN RESOURCES Dina Nathanson
SENIOR VICE PRESIDENT, CHIEF COMMUNICATIONS OFFICER Erica Jensen
VICE CHAIRMAN Mell Meredith Frazier

For the Love of Restaurants

A GRIZZLED RESTAURANT CRITIC once advised me "not to join the Army in order to cover it," but by then I was already in too deep–I'd been embedded in restaurants since I was 18 years old, starting with a gig making sandwiches at Jersey Mike's in Chapel Hill, North Carolina. For the next 12 years, I went back and forth between working in restaurants and newspaper newsrooms before I chose the media business full time. What I learned about restaurant people during my time in professional kitchens–that they're creative, scrappy, big-hearted, and resilient–has only solidified during my four years at the helm of *Food & Wine*. It's one of the reasons I look forward every year to the making of this annual Restaurant Issue, where we celebrate the people and places you should seek out next.

This includes, of course, the 33rd class of *Food & Wine* Best New Chefs. Since 1988, our editors have sought out the most exciting up-and-coming culinary talent in America. The first class included future luminaries like Thomas Keller and Daniel Boulud. We're confident that this year's class will also leave their stamp on American cuisine. To find them, Restaurant Editor Khushbu Shah spent seven weeks looking not only for the most dynamic cooking in the country, but also for chefs who are leading with respect, intent on changing the culture of restaurants for those who work in them as well as for those who dine. (Big thanks to Khushbu and our creative team, led by Photo Director Tori Katherman and Creative Director Winslow Taft, for creating the look for this year's feature.) Turn to p. 125 to meet the 2021 F&W Best New Chefs and read about their favorite spots to eat and drink in the cities they call home. We hope their stories and recommendations inspire your next big night out.

This year's class of chefs is all the more remarkable for delivering excellence during a pandemic that has gutted the industry. As the BNCs and their peers continue to reinvent what it means to run a restaurant by putting their team members first, we focused on a fundamental question that doesn't get asked enough: What are the diner's responsibilities in the hospitality equation? The answers, informed by months of reporting and a survey of your fellow readers, can be found in "The New Rules of Dining Out" on p. 46.

You don't have to have worked in restaurants to love them–or even to cover them. But we all have work to do to become better customers in this new era of hospitality.

HUNTER LEWIS
HUNTER@FOODANDWINE.COM

Eight Great Bites
Some of my favorite food memories from the road this year

NAMI NORI, NEW YORK CITY

Chef de cuisine Jihan Lee's **sushi hand rolls,** including a tuna, fluke, caviar, uni, and black truffle one, stacked on top of warm seasoned rice and wrapped in crunchy nori, are the best bites I've eaten this year.

CARNE MARE, NEW YORK CITY

The sleeper hit is 2000 F&W Best New Chef Andrew Carmellini's tender and funky **Gorgonzola-cured Wagyu strip loin,** sure to be imitated by chefs across the country.

L'INDUSTRIE PIZZERIA, BROOKLYN

The pizzaiolos at the recently expanded slice joint L'industrie are turning out some of my favorite pizza in New York right now. Order the **spicy salami slice** with **hot honey.**

HORN BARBECUE, OAKLAND, CALIFORNIA

Of course you should order 2021 F&W BNC Matt Horn's slices of jiggly **brisket,** but don't sleep on his **jalapeño sausage,** oozing with cheddar (order an extra link for a breakfast hash the next day), or the sides, especially his **mac and cheese.** Read more about chef Horn on p. 128.

GREYFIELD INN, CUMBERLAND ISLAND, GEORGIA

Greyfield, a secluded base camp for nature adventurers, is unlike any place on earth. Chef Jada Veljkov makes every ingredient count in dishes like crispy, juicy **porchetta** and a standout **shrimp and grits.**

BOMBERA, OAKLAND, CALIFORNIA

No bells and whistles here, just really nice folks serving the food of Mexico and California in an old fire station. You'll want two orders of the **taquitos** and extra bags of chef-owner Dominica Rice-Cisneros' thick, salty **tortilla chips and guacamole.**

VALLEY BAR AND BOTTLE, SONOMA, CALIFORNIA

The Valley team turns out pure and soulful cooking from a pocket-size kitchen, including **stewed shelling beans with sumac** and a **seeded green goddess salad.**

MAIZ DE LA VIDA AND CHOPPER, NASHVILLE

This power pop-up duo featuring a masa specialist and a cocktail bar makes for a fun afternoon in East Nashville. Try the **vegetable taco** from Maiz de la Vida's food truck with a pitch-perfect **piña colada** from the tiki bar, Chopper.

Subscription Help: *foodandwine.com/myaccount* or email us at *FAWcustserv@cdsfulfillment.com* or call *1-800-333-6569.*

photography by RAMONA ROSALES

CHEERS TO THESE STARS

Congratulations to the Best New Chefs

OBSESSIONS

Best Bites of 2021 From a TikTok-inspired wrap to butter terrine, these dishes stood out this year.

By Khushbu Shah

IT RETAINS ALL THE GOOEY, MELTY CHEESE MAGIC, BUT WITH A SLIGHTLY NUTTIER FLAVOR.

▲ **CRISPY PROVOLONE**

OSPI, LOS ANGELES

IN JACKSON KALB'S evolution of the mozzarella stick, provolone replaces mozzarella, and the deep-fried appetizer is supersized into a puck large enough for two. It retains all the gooey, melty cheese magic, but with a slightly nuttier flavor. Kalb serves it with a mouthwatering vodka sauce that made me wonder why deep-fried cheese is ever served with anything else.

SEE ALASKA
WITH THE BEST

Dreaming of seeing the Great Land? Trust the cruise line voted Best in Alaska. As one of the few with access to Glacier Bay National Park & Preserve, we offer more itineraries that include this UNESCO World Heritage Site than any other cruise line. Our spacious, uncrowded ships are known for award-winning dining, the best live music at sea, and service that brings guests back again and again. And, only Holland America Line offers culinary-themed excursions in partnership with *FOOD & WINE*. Extend your adventure to our own resort at Denali National Park and even explore the Yukon's gold rush history. We've shown guests the majesty of Alaska for 75 years, and we'd love to show you as well.

Have It All with our best amenities included in your fare: Shore Excursions, Drink Package, Specialty Dining and Wi-Fi!*

Call your Travel Advisor or 1-877-SAIL HAL, or visit hollandamerica.com

BEST IN ALASKA

AFAR Travelers' Awards 2020
PORTHOLE Best Itineraries 2020
TRAVEL AGE WEST Wave Awards 2020
CRUISE CRITIC Cruisers' Choice 2019

Holland America Line®
SAVOR THE JOURNEY

BUTTER TERRINE

LUTIE'S, AUSTIN

I AUDIBLY GASPED each time I encountered this butter terrine, first gently melting on a stack of pancakes, and again when it arrived on a plate as part of the bread service at Lutie's. Chefs Bradley Nicholson and Susana Querejazu alternate layers of cultured and brown butter in a pan, chill it until it's solid, and then cut slices off of the terrine to reveal a beautiful slab of striped butter that adds a multitude of flavor to any dish.

CHEFS BRADLEY NICHOLSON AND SUSANA QUEREJAZU ALTERNATE LAYERS OF CULTURED AND BROWN BUTTER.

TOP TRENDS

VIETNAMESE DESSERTS GET THEIR DUE

Vietnamese desserts—heavy on ingredients like condensed milk, pandan, coconut, and coffee—are finally getting their time in the spotlight thanks to dishes like the chewy pandan waffles at Berlu in Portland, Oregon, and the crispy black sesame ube cookies from Bạn Bè in New York City.

PHOTOGRAPHY: CEDRIC ANGELES
ILLUSTRATIONS: SILVIA TACK

THE OUTER LAYER SHATTERS WITH EACH BITE, REVEALING TENDER, MOIST MEAT.

▲ **GA CHIEN**

MOON RABBIT,
WASHINGTON, D.C.

WE ARE LIVING through a fried chicken renaissance. The sheer amount of excellent fried chicken available across the country is overwhelming, but at his new restaurant, Moon Rabbit, chef Kevin Tien (a 2018 *Food & Wine* Best New Chef) makes a version that stands out from the crowd—and not just because he serves the meat still attached to the bird's claws. The ga chien pulls from Tien's Vietnamese heritage and is lacquered in a chile-maple fish sauce, almost as if the chicken has been candied. The outer layer shatters with each bite, revealing tender, moist meat.

FIESTA SPAGHETTI

POGIBOY, WASHINGTON, D.C.

THIS CHEFFY RIFF on the Filipino fast food classic from Jollibee is the ideal comfort meal. Chefs Tom Cunanan and Paolo Dungca toss al dente spaghetti with a Bolognese made from hot dogs and shower it with melty Gouda cheese. It's deeply savory but also has a punch of sweetness from the banana ketchup in the sauce. What's not to love about a giant plate of carbs covered in cheese and tossed with slices of bright pink hot dogs? It's a dish that doesn't take itself too seriously, but just seriously enough to be the best version out there.

GIM-BAP SUPREME

TOKI, PORTLAND, OREGON

I NEVER THOUGHT one of my favorite dishes of the year would be inspired by a TikTok trend. Chef Peter Cho decided to do his own version of the "wrap" video, where tortillas are divided into four quadrants, topped with four different ingredients, folded on top of each other, and griddled. He uses a square of nori as his base, layering each quadrant with rice, ribbons of egg, and veggies like carrots and purple cabbage. Cho stuffs the center of the gim-bap with tempura-fried nori for crunch. It's served with a deceptively simple sauce of tamarind and French's mustard.

TOP TRENDS

VEGGIE CUTOUTS MAKE THE ROUNDS

Forget knife skills like julienne and brunoise: The hippest way to cut vegetables these days is with a small cookie cutter. Chefs at Moon Rabbit in Washington, D.C., and Naemo in Los Angeles are punching shapes likes flowers, hearts, and stars out of carrots, cucumbers, and radishes to add a playful pop to their dishes.

◀

PAPLET FRY
DHAMAKA, NEW YORK CITY

DHAMAKA MIGHT BE the best Indian restaurant in the country right now, and it's definitely the most interesting. The menu is dedicated to underrepresented regional dishes that aren't commonly found in the West, and the sleeper hit is the paplet fry. It's a dish of pomfret, a delicate butterfish, that chef Chintan Pandya marinates with garlic paste, turmeric, red chile powder, and ginger and then fries until golden. The result is a succulent and flaky fish that's easy to tear with your hands.

▲

SHRIMP AND PROSCIUTTO TORTELLINI
KIMIKA, NEW YORK CITY

DON'T CALL THIS FUSION, but instead a masterful partnership between the Italian dish of tortellini in brodo and ozoni, a Japanese New Year soup made with mochi. Plump tortellini are stuffed with salty prosciutto and tender shrimp, only to float in a pool of crystal clear dashi. The bowl is finished off with slices of pink-rimmed kamaboko (fish cakes) and thinly sliced scallions. It's a playground of textures that's just really fun to eat.

TOP TRENDS

FULLY VEGAN ASIAN CONCEPTS

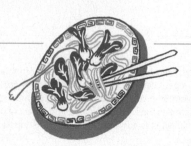

Chefs are doubling down on plant-based menus that also bring their cultures to life. Find vegan Chinese food at Fat Choy in New York City, vegan Sri Lankan cooking at Mirisata in Portland, Oregon, and vegan Singaporean-inspired options at Lion Dance Cafe in Oakland, California.

UNCORK EXTRAORDINARY.™

Decanter®
HIGHLY
RECOMMENDED
92
POINTS

Santa Margherita

PROSECCO SUPERIORE
VALDOBBIADENE DOCG

THE CAKE TASTES JUST
AS STUNNING AS IT LOOKS: AIRY
LAYERS OF OLIVE OIL CHIFFON
CAKE AND SWOOPS OF
FIG LEAF CREAM.

OLIVE OIL
CHIFFON
CAKE

BAYOU SAINT CAKE,
NEW ORLEANS

BEFORE I FINALLY made it to New Orleans, I had stalked Bronwen Wyatt's cakes on Instagram @bayousaintcake for months, wistfully staring at the vast array of edible flowers and squiggles of buttercream that adorn each. Wyatt is part of an ongoing movement of pastry chefs who have left restaurants and are selling incredible baked goods directly to customers. The cake tastes just as stunning as it looks: airy layers of olive oil chiffon cake, swoops of fig leaf cream, and rose and geranium preserves. The whole thing is enveloped in a tangy crème fraîche buttercream and decorated with her signature buttercream twists and turns. And yes, I took a million photos of it before I dug in.

DREAM IN CAYMAN.

CAYMAN ISLANDS
GRAND CAYMAN | CAYMAN BRAC | LITTLE CAYMAN

VisitCaymanIslands.com

BEST EATS IN CHARLESTON

Voted by *Food+Wine* readers among the **World's Best Cities for Food**, Charleston offers a diverse dining scene that will tempt your taste buds and nourish your soul. Read up on these culinary experiences and chart your own tasty adventures.

___

COASTAL CUISINE

From neighborhood spots to upscale restaurants, fresh seafood is a local staple and fall marks the start of oyster season on the South Carolina coast. Slurp oysters at swanky eateries housed in repurposed buildings dating back to the 1920s, and soak up the casual ambiance of the **Oyster Shed at Leon's**. On the waterfront, **Fleet Landing** is a top pick for sustainable seafood and maritime style. Try the iron skillet mussels or chilled blue crab dip.

REGIONAL FLAVORS

Explore a melting pot of Southern, Gullah, and Lowcountry cuisine, which mingles West African, French, English, and Caribbean flavors. Settle in for a modern take on Southern recipes at **Husk** or sample authentic Gullah dishes that have been passed down for generations. Get familiar with Lowcountry standards like she-crab soup, and dig into a helping of shrimp-and-grits at a classic diner.

CRAFT BREWS

To go along with savory eats, check out the **Charleston Ale Trail** and the impressive beer scene with around 30 breweries. Head to **Holy Brewing** to familiarize yourself with irreverently named beers like Overly Friendly IPA. Their beers pair perfectly with savory pizza and Charleston has a surprisingly good pie scene. Sample what's on tap in a pint, half pint, or flight at **Frothy Beard Brewing** or pop over to **Johns Island** and check out local breweries.

▶ *Shop, eat, and relax in Charleston with the Capital One Venture card. For more information, go to **capitalone.com**.*

Capital One
What's in your wallet?

Unlimited double miles.
Unlimited destinations.

With the Capital One Venture card, you can earn
unlimited double miles wherever you shop and
redeem them on any travel purchase.

The Traveling Kitchen How to cook, drink, and entertain better in your vacation rental

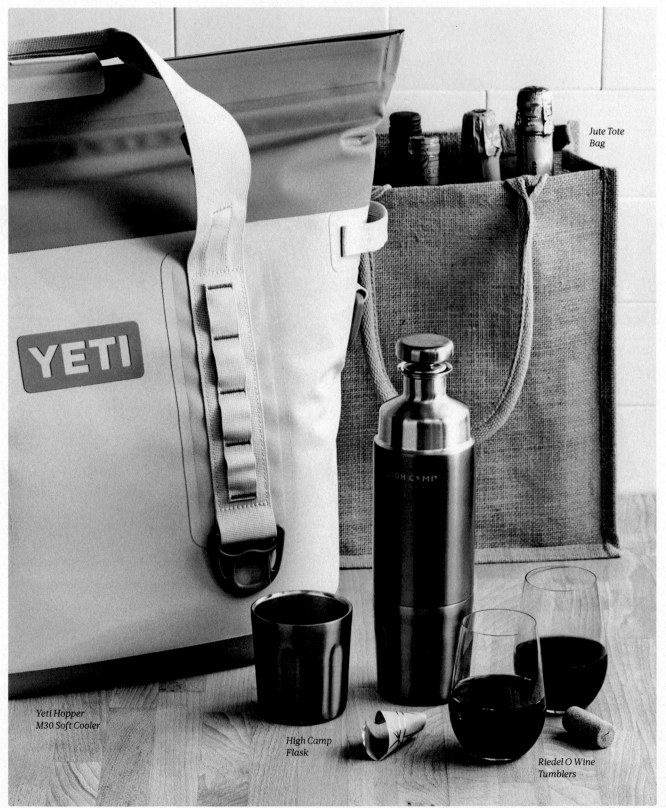

Jute Tote Bag

Yeti Hopper
M30 Soft Cooler

High Camp
Flask

Riedel O Wine
Tumblers

photography by VICTOR PROTASIO

SAY 'GOOD MORNING' AND ACTUALLY MEAN IT

WHAT COFFEE IS MEANT TO BE

NESPRESSO®

Atmos Vacuum Canister

AeroPress Coffee Maker

Elemental spices

Messermeister Adventure Folding Knife

EVEN BEFORE the Great Disruption of 2020 necessitated short trips closer to home, one of my superpowers was booking vacation rentals that met (or exceeded, even!) my every whim. I'm that person who trawls booking sites for hours on end, poring over every detail of a listing, its photos, and reviews. I look for design-forward interiors and curation with character, lots and lots of natural light, a comfy bed, generous entertaining spaces–but above all, a well-equipped kitchen.

I've especially honed this skill during the past year. With international travel off the cards and a cautious avoidance of planes and hotels, my husband and I took to the road. What kinds of things did we look for in listings before we booked? Beyond the obvious descriptors, there are a few key giveaways in photos that point to a thoughtful kitchen space: a stand mixer, a lineup of sharp-looking knives on a magnetized rack on the wall, the brand of cooking appliances, an ample-looking spice rack and pantry, and Dutch ovens, cast-iron, or enamelware on open shelving. We'd also read all the reviews, looking for specific comments about the kitchen, hoping that other food nerds would offer us valuable clues.

Naturally, there's only so much you can plan for, but one small insurance policy is to bring a few useful things with you. It comes as no surprise that many on the F&W team are just like me, keen to cook with local produce and eat delicious things while on vacation. Here is a collection of our go-to tools we take with us on the road to ensure cooking is always a pleasure. –*MELANIE HANSCHE*

AEROPRESS COFFEE MAKER

Caffeine fiends who prefer a better brew than what a French press can offer know to travel with a small, lightweight Aero-Press. Get the reusable Fellow Prismo filter attachment and do away with single-use filters. (*$30, aeropress.com; $25, fellowproducts.com*)

ATMOS VACUUM CANISTER

Use these Atmos canisters to transport coffee beans, loose-leaf tea, cereal, or marshmallows. The lid never comes off by accident, and the air pumps out of them to seal in your ingredients, keeping them super fresh. (*$30, fellowproducts.com*)

MESSERMEISTER ADVENTURE FOLDING KNIFE

For the past eight years, my go-to knife has been a Messermeister. I used to wrap it in a dish towel to transport it; luckily, they released a six-inch foldable version, ideal for trips and camping. (*$80, messermeister.com*)

ELEMENTAL SPICES

It's wise to travel with a few seasonings that will work with local ingredients wherever you go. Burlap & Barrel's garlic powder adds savory depth to marinades, and Spiceology's rosemary-Dijon rub perks up meats. (*$8, burlapandbarrel .com; $14, spiceology.com*)

RIEDEL O WINE TUMBLERS

The last rental I booked had an exceptional kitchen, but only cumbersome tumblers—not great for the lovely wines we brought along with us. I always bring a box of these stemless glasses in the car for exactly this reason. (*$33 for two, riedel.com*)

HIGH CAMP FIRELIGHT 750 FLASK

I generally premix a batch of Negronis and take them in a glass mason jar, but this is a much safer way to transport your batched cocktails and has fancy tumblers included. Also, no leaks—this thing seals tight! (*$125, highcampflasks.com*)

YETI HOPPER M30 SOFT COOLER

Being a traveler means bringing home tasty stuff for later, like local cheeses, charcuterie, or veggies. A soft, insulated cooler bag that keeps everything chilled down for hours is key, like this hardcore Yeti cooler bag. (*$300, yeti.com*)

JUTE TOTE BAG

My husband is in the wine trade and has been using these totes for years to cart bottles to wine tastings. They come with bottle dividers that store flat. Simple, sturdy, and inexpensive, they fit nicely behind a car's seat. (*$7, totebagfactory.com*)

LUXURIOUSLY APPROACHABLE

JUSTIN's Cabernet Sauvignon is America's #1 luxury Cabernet due to the bold flavors derived from our artisanal approach and the naturally limestone-rich soil of Paso Robles, California. Every bottle is crafted with care— hand-harvesting, hand-sorting, and oak barrel aging—to produce a balanced, elevated red.

Exceptional from every angle.

JUSTIN

CABERNET SAUVIGNON

PASO ROBLES

justinwine.com

THE INNOVATOR

Pizza with Purpose
Chef Kurt Evans is paving new paths to the kitchen for formerly incarcerated folks. By Abigail Glasgow

FOR KURT EVANS, chefs are akin to first responders who meet an urgent social need to make an impact. In his case, that need is decarceration in the United States. "I have experienced mass incarceration through friends and family members," he says; his mission is to positively impact returning citizens.

Evans grew up in Philadelphia, shadowing his grandmother in the kitchen. "She would say, 'I'm going to show you how to make this once, so you better get it,'" he says with a laugh. Needless to say, he did. From an early career start alongside Robert and Benjamin Bynum, whom Evans praises as the longest-tenured Black restaurateurs in Philly, Evans has become an authority in what he calls Black heritage cooking. He makes a mean fish and grits, but what he values most are the sociopolitical undertones innate to serving and sharing food.

"Black people, we've always strategized over food," he explains. "Slaves plotted their escape over meals. Georgia Gilmore literally sold platters out of her home to bail people out of jail during the bus boycott movements. Leah Chase fed everyone from Martin Luther King Jr. to Barack Obama."

Inspired by the dinners South Philly Barbacoa's Cristina Martinez and Benjamin Miller hosted that centered around the challenges facing undocumented workers, Evans built his own series called End Mass Incarceration. His first dinner took place in Philadelphia on January 13, 2018, and brought together formerly incarcerated speakers with the likes of Nina Ahmad, who was running for auditor general at the time. Having individuals present who were candidates for office–people who could enact policy that might positively impact those inside–created a setting where district attorneys might find themselves passing beans to kids straight out of Rikers.

While the dinner series aims to bridge the social and educational gap between the formerly incarcerated and those distanced from the system, Evans also wanted to build something to directly employ returning citizens. "I bought into a restaurant called Route 23 in Philly, and I remember one day, three employees were visited by their parole officers. I thought, 'This is such a simple way to help ... If we don't hire them, who will?'"

In March 2021, Evans opened Down North Pizza in North Philadelphia, a restaurant wherein all eight employees are formerly incarcerated. "The food industry has never had a problem hiring formerly incarcerated people. The problem is employers threatening to call parole officers and dehumanizing these guys," Evans says. At Down North, employees are paid above minimum wage, tips are pooled, and the team avoids traditional titles to eliminate any hierarchy.

Evans is now in the process of signing over his ownership interests to Down North's employees–it's on to the next endeavor. One is an extension of Everybody Eats, the nonprofit he cofounded during the COVID-19 pandemic. At the time, some neighborhoods were witnessing what he called a "food apartheid" because of vandalism resulting from unrest following George Floyd's murder. "We delivered over 1,200 chef-prepared meals," he says. Now, they're building a new arm. "When Bobby Seale ran for mayor in Oakland in '73, he would give out produce and canned goods to get individuals registered to vote." This year, Everybody Eats will launch a food truck where Evans and his partners will be giving out produce to Philadelphia residents.

"Everybody's using the word 'reimagining,' but nobody's really reimagining anything," he says. A world with more of Evans' food and fewer people in prison certainly sounds like a future to get behind.

PITCH IN

Support Kurt Evans' work via Everybody Eats at everybodyeats philly.org/donate.

PHOTOGRAPHY: COURTESY OF KURT EVANS

Awaken

Enhance your wellbeing at
a secluded island retreat

SENSEI LĀNAʻI

A FOUR SEASONS RESORT

SENSEI.COM
808.468.7833

Lānaʻi, Hawaiʻi

ON MEDIA

Origin Stories This fall's most anticipated food books trace their authors' love of food back to their roots.

By Jamila Robinson

THROUGH DEEPLY PERSONAL MEMOIRS and compelling biographies, this fall's new releases feature authors, celebrity chefs, and industry personalities delivering a sharp view of why they cook–and behave–as they do.

Host of CNN's *Searching for Italy* Stanley Tucci shared his obsession with Italian food with two previous cookbooks, but his forthcoming memoir, *Taste: My Life Through Food* ($28, Gallery Books), takes readers to the beginning of this love affair with cooking, both as a child and later as an actor in food-related films like *Big Night* and *Julie & Julia*. Similarly, in *You Had Me at Pét-Nat* ($28, Hachette), independent magazine publisher Rachel Signer explains how she became consumed by the allure of natural wines, first as a journalist and waitress in Brooklyn and later after falling in love and relocating to South Australia.

Even the familiar stories give way to twists when read from a different perspective. Laurie Woolever, a writer and editor who was Anthony Bourdain's longtime assistant, uses quotes to bring readers deeper into his world in *Bourdain: The Definitive Oral Biography* ($30, Ecco).

JAMILA RECOMMENDS

The Red Boat Fish Sauce Cookbook **by Cuong Pham, Tien Nguyen, and Diep Tran**
Cuong Pham, founder of the popular condiment company, offers his immigrant story, which includes fleeing Vietnam after the war, his connection to Apple founder Steve Jobs, and his ongoing quest to honor his mother's cooking. *($25, Mariner Books)*

Black Food **by Bryant Terry**
This compilation curated by author and chef Bryant Terry is a celebration of Black culture that weaves food with African origins through poetry, essays, and artwork. *($40, 4 Color Books)*

Taste Makers: Seven Immigrant Women Who Revolutionized Food in America **by Mayukh Sen**
James Beard Award–winning writer Mayukh Sen presents portraits of women in food, including Italian cookbook author Marcella Hazan and Norma Shirley, a culinary giant of Jamaica. *($27, W.W. Norton & Company)*

Through details shared by his friends and family, we learn more about Bourdain's kind heart, how much he wanted to be a writer, his habit of fidgeting when he was uncomfortable, and the dark world he inhabited, especially when traveling.

The season's cookbooks echo the trend of origin-story memoirs with recipes that underscore the writers' influences from family and pop culture, and their motivations. The worldwide obsession with the *Great British Bake Off* franchise has made Nadiya Hussain and Vallery Lomas (via the American version) popular food influencers with highly anticipated baking books, both of which offer recipes for comforting cakes and ambitious pithiviers. But it is in the personal essays and headnotes that both Hussain and Lomas illustrate how baking became the center of their lives, and the lifestyle and career choices they made to be on the TV show. Those backstories are also what make cookbooks like *Treasures of the Mexican Table* ($35, Mariner Books) by PBS veteran Pati Jinich more personal and useful. Her motivation for her latest book? To highlight the culinary diversity of Mexico and the ingredients from her home country's 32 states.

Ultimately, taking readers back to the beginning helps to build connections to pop culture and provides context for our behavior. In *The Secret History of Food* ($28, Ecco), writer Matt Siegel offers up irreverent looks at some of our favorite foods, like chiles, ice cream, and tomatoes. He also dives into concepts like Americans' need for plenty of grocery store choices, the ways stylists make food more attractive and sensual by using the same tools used by the adult film industry (hence the term "food porn"), and the universal use of food words like "honey" and "pumpkin" as terms of endearment. By exploring the etymology of foods like honey, we have a better understanding of what it means to call someone sweet.

illustration by MIGUEL ÁNGEL CAMPRUBÍ

YETI BUILT FOR THE WILD.

THE NEW RULES

How to become a five-star restaurant guest in the new era of hospitality

PRODUCED BY
HUNTER LEWIS

ILLUSTRATIONS BY
FRANZ LANG

OF DINING OUT

Dining out this spring after my second COVID-19 vaccine jab felt a little like clipping a climbing rope onto a harness and walking out to a rock ledge with a thousand-foot drop. Will this thing really keep me safe?

This spring, as the country began to reopen, I took public health guidance from the CDC and mask-wearing cues from restaurant staff. Restaurant Editor Khushbu Shah came off the road after scouting the 2021 class of *Food & Wine* Best New Chefs (p. 125) about the time when I began to rappel off the rock and dine out in earnest. Even though a few experiences proved frustrating, they ultimately rekindled my love for the people who work in restaurants.

Dining out right now sometimes means that we're left to our own devices, quite literally. This summer in New York City, while entering a new cocktail bar known for its fried chicken sandwich, I filled out a QR code–generated contact-tracing form on my phone. The server told me the kitchen was closing soon and asked me to order quickly via another QR code, a tiny pixelated sticker on a tiny black bottle of hand sanitizer. The venue was so dark that I had to hold the bottle up to a lamp in order to pull up the menu on my phone. Then, I had to shout my order through my mask so the server could hear it over the loud music. Cue the tiny violin.

A few nights later, I joined friends and colleagues for dinner at Francie, a Brooklyn spot known for its signature roast duck and one of the last cheese carts in the city. We sat down in a cushy banquette, ordered from an actual paper menu, and spent a few joyful hours catching up on life and work. After the rocky experience a few nights before, the quality of food, wine, and service reminded me that the root word of *restaurant* is the Latin *restaurare*, to renew. For the first time in weeks, I forgot about those invisible climbing ropes keeping me and other diners safe. As we said our goodbyes and walked out the door, we thanked every staffer in sight.

Then, during the editing of this story, the delta variant reared its head. In late July, the Biden administration and the CDC changed policy and recommended that vaccinated people wear masks inside again. New York City made proof of vaccination mandatory to enter gyms and restaurants. I'm back on the ledge looking over the precipice and wondering what comes next.

When we surveyed *Food & Wine* readers this summer (see "2021 *Food & Wine* Reader Survey," at right), 86% of you were dining out an average of three times per week.

Chances are we've all had some similar experiences this year. But what about the people cooking and serving our food and pouring our drinks? How are they faring? The answer: not great. We may feel more freedom than last year, but the spaces we're entering have fundamentally changed, and so have the lives of those who operate, manage, and work in them.

COVID-19 hit the restaurant industry with the force of a hurricane. While many of us were cooking at home seven nights a week during lockdown, many bars and restaurants were struggling to stay afloat. Approximately 90,000 closed. Global supply chain issues have created shortages of staples like ketchup, forcing some restaurateurs to shorten menus and raise prices. Foods like grains, meat, and poultry cost more now. So does labor. And the COVID-19 protocols and equipment meant to keep us and workers safe add expenses.

The second wave of that hurricane brought reckonings on the issues of race, gender, and equity in the workplace. Some chef-owners, like Ravi Kapur in San Francisco and Katie Button in Asheville, North Carolina, reacted by retooling their business models in order to pay their employees fairer wages. Other restaurateurs reopened with a Before Times back-to-business mentality and have struggled to find workers. Even though hundreds of thousands of jobs have been added to the restaurant and bar sector since February, the hospitality industry was still down 1.3 million jobs, or 10%, in June compared to pre-pandemic levels, according to data from the Bureau of Labor Statistics. Food service workers are leaving for other industries. Nearly 6% of them quit their jobs in May, the highest number in decades, according to *The Wall Street Journal*. Restaurant Instagram accounts now double as job recruiting sites. Signing bonuses and perks that were unheard of when I was a $10-an-hour line cook in the early aughts have become the new normal. How tight is the labor market in Birmingham, Alabama, where I live? A restaurateur friend of mine offered his cooks $1,200 to find a dishwasher; none could.

We've heard, from dozens of restaurant workers during our reporting over the past 18 months, that customers became more entitled during the pandemic. Diner behavior continues to rankle.

The truth is that every one of us plays an important role in the hospitality equation. Hospitality shouldn't be purely transactional; kindness shouldn't be a one-way street flowing only from workers toward guests. This guide was designed to help all of us navigate a new and rapidly evolving era of hospitality, offering context and advice on everything from tipping and reservations to dietary restrictions and phone usage. It may take years for restaurants to regain their footing. Meantime, we can all do our part to be better guests.

—HUNTER LEWIS

> *It may take years for restaurants to regain their footing. Meantime, we can all do our part to be better guests.*

2021 FOOD & WINE READER SURVEY

DINING OUT FREQUENCY

86% of F&W consumers are currently dining out an average of three times a week and primarily in independent and neighborhood restaurants.

The number of F&W readers ordering takeout or delivery an average of twice a week. **75%**

34% of readers say they will return to pre-pandemic takeout/delivery levels.

F&W READERS' PET PEEVES

Poor attitude and rushed service are the top pet peeves that F&W readers have with restaurant waitstaff.

Poor attitude	93%	
Rushing	89%	
Not fully engaged	73%	
Inconsistent service	69%	
Slow service	64%	

BEHAVIOR

73% of F&W readers would be willing to sign a diner code of conduct.

Only 26% want to use QR codes to view menus in the future.

RESTAURANT WORKERS' PET PEEVES*

Insufficient tipping	84%	
Not disclosing dietary restrictions up front	84%	
Refusal to follow COVID safety guidelines	82%	
No-show reservations	81%	
Attitude toward staff	77%	

*From June 7–13, 2021, 1,500 F&W readers responded to this study. It's important to note that only 81 restaurant industry professionals responded, however. We're including their pet peeves here for reference, but the low sample size does not give an accurate comparison to readers' pet peeves.

Our Apologies, But the Customer Is Not Always Right

CONDENSED FROM REPORTING BY **RESTAURANT EDITOR KHUSHBU SHAH**

RESTAURANT WORKERS HAVE ALWAYS SWAPPED STORIES about customer entitlement: the ridiculous demands, the difficult guests, the bad tippers. But the pandemic and the behavior that came with it–impatience regarding wait times, name-calling, frustration over limited seating and menu choices, disregard for safety protocols–only serves to highlight how pervasive the problem really is. These blunt expressions of entitlement are rooted in the popular adage "The customer is always right," a notion that started in department stores in the early 1900s and now sits at the center of American hospitality. "We've taught the American diner that there are no boundaries, that they can ask for anything and everything, and that it should be given to them," says Lauren Friel, the owner of Rebel Rebel in Somerville, Massachusetts. Service today is transactional and commodified, says Miguel de Leon, wine director at Pinch Chinese in NYC. "It becomes about what the restaurant can do for the diner," he explains. In her 2020 book *Be My Guest*, Priya Basil writes: "The hospitality industry ... thrives on the message that you are the only one who counts: you should come first, your every need considered and catered to. You deserve it, after all, as long as you can pay." But now, that sensibility seems–both to restaurant professionals and, honestly, to most diners–outdated, a servile relic of a former (pre-pandemic) time.

Averaged out, F&W readers believe a tip should be

↓

21%

17% believe that a standard tip should be

↓

25%

Average tip for delivery should be 18%, according to readers.

Takeout tips should be about 15%, they say.

48%

are interested in paying a mandatory 18%–20% service fee built into the bill in lieu of tipping.

79%

are willing to pay a COVID-19 surcharge.

2.

Tip Big

CONDENSED FROM REPORTING BY **REGAN STEPHENS**

→ **YOUR TIPS MATTER NOW MORE THAN EVER.** "As restaurants cater to growing demands with the return of normalcy, many places are navigating how to meet this surge in demand with limited staff. So do remember to tip–and a bit more than you might have in the past," says Paula DaSilva, executive chef at Burlock Coast at The Ritz-Carlton, Fort Lauderdale. If you thought of 20% as the ceiling for your tip in the Before Times, start thinking of that now as the floor. "Before the pandemic, 20% was seen as an appropriate tip for exceptional service," says Shayn Prapaisilp, owner of Chao Baan in St. Louis. "Right now, 20% should be the minimum." That goes for when you're at a sit-down restaurant, but also for staff when you're getting takeout and drivers (who sometimes earn as little as $2 an hour) when you're getting food delivered.

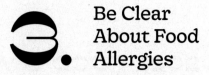

3.

Be Clear About Food Allergies

CONDENSED FROM REPORTING BY **SENIOR EDITOR KAT KINSMAN**

→ **ABOUT 32 MILLION** Americans have food allergies, and every three minutes, a food-related allergic reaction sends someone to the ER, according to FARE (foodallergy.org), a nonprofit devoted to education and research regarding food allergies. And, says chef and restaurateur Ming Tsai, responsibility for guests' well-being falls both on the restaurant staff and on diners. Tsai became a spokesperson for the Food Allergy and Anaphylaxis Network when his son was diagnosed with a severe peanut allergy. Intimately acquainted with the stakes as both a chef and a father, Tsai later decided to write an "allergy bible" that he uses at his own restaurant, Blue Dragon; he also provides templates on his website (ming.com) for others to create their own versions.

So what's the bottom line for diners? Overcommunicate, Tsai says. Call the restaurant manager ahead of time, and make notes in the reservation app you're using. When you arrive, remind the staff again. What not to do? Don't say you have a food allergy if what you actually have is an intolerance, restriction, or simple aversion. If you don't like green peppers, just tell your server that you prefer not to eat them; don't claim that they'll send you to the hospital. As Tsai says, "Nothing pisses a chef off more than when we bend over backwards, change our cutting boards, tongs, and gloves, because they've said they have a dairy allergy–and then we see them eating an ice cream dessert."

Use Your Phone for Memories, Not Calls

4.

BY **KORSHA WILSON**

→ **DIVISIVE AT FIRST,** cell phones in restaurants are now an inevitable part of dining out, and the reality is that tech can help diners engage with a restaurant more deeply. For Christine Sahadi Whelan, managing partner of Sahadi's in Brooklyn's Industry City, it's about meeting each guest at their "comfort level with tech," she says. "I was worried people wouldn't engage with one another, but they're actually doing it in a really organic way." Whether they're using QR codes to pull up the menu, creating Instagram stories about their meals, or just snapping a picture of a favorite dish, diners are creating memories over dinner in a restaurant via tech. That's a good thing, Whelan says. But there is one cardinal rule she doesn't bend on: "I do want you to turn off your ringer, though."

5.

People of America, Respect That Reservation!

CONDENSED FROM REPORTING BY
SENIOR EDITOR MARIA YAGODA AND
**JOHN WINTERMAN, OWNER OF
FRANCIE IN BROOKLYN**

→ **SHOW UP. FULL STOP.** Restaurants simply cannot sustain the financial losses of no-shows, particularly right now. "Diners who book need to show up for their reservation in a timely fashion or to cancel in a timely fashion. This is a tangible show of support for your restaurant community," says John Winterman, co-owner of Francie in Brooklyn. In non-pandemic times, a restaurant might have a waiting list, people at the bar, or last-minute requests coming in, all of which could help mitigate the loss of a no-show. But "in the current climate, a lost reservation is just that: lost, irretrievable, irreplaceable," Winterman says. "The night a party of six no-showed on their three-weeks-ago booking, that represented 20% of what we had planned on for that evening. This lack of manners and–I'll say it–complete lack of character seriously impacts our staff, not only financially but also in terms of morale."

If you use reservation apps like OpenTable or Resy, don't abuse them. Mark Strausman of Mark's Off Madison in New York City says that even though these apps have made life smoother for guests, some people use them to double-book tables or repeatedly no-show. "It's just one more example of digital convenience making it easier to forget that there are actual humans behind the business," he says. If you can't show up for your reservation (life does happen), always call the restaurant and let them know with as much notice as possible.

RESERVATION REALITIES

45%

of F&W readers most frequently use dining reservation apps to secure a table when dining out.

↓

31%

call the restaurant directly.

20%

show up and wait for a table.

ONLY
5%

of those polled said they had not shown up for a reservation.

6.

Patience, Patience, Patience

BY **REGAN STEPHENS**

→ **REMEMBER LAST FALL,** when kitchen burnout snuck up on us? Without unfettered access, we learned just how much we appreciated restaurants. But as that sense of gratitude has waned, even while the pandemic hasn't, chefs are urging diners to be patient. Labor shortages "put pressure on current employees to carry longer hours and to do tasks they have not received proper training for," says Gabriella Valls of Ponyboy in Brooklyn. As a result, service might look different than it did in the past. Also contributing to this new reality are the ever-changing COVID-19 safety guidelines that make Andre Fowles of Miss Lily's in New York City feel like "you're opening a new restaurant every week." Shifting outdoor and indoor layouts also makes replenishing silverware from a waiter station or delivering food to your table take longer. "When we designed the restaurant, we didn't think about having another 30 seats outdoors," says Cédric Vongerichten, owner of NYC's Wayan. All of these hurdles make it harder to offer diners the experience they expect. It doesn't mean restaurants aren't trying, though.

7.

Smaller Menus Are the Order of the Day

BY **REGAN STEPHENS**

➡ **YOU MAY HAVE NOTICED PARED-DOWN MENUS.** For starters, blame staffing shortages. "Even just one less cook at night eliminates an entire station," says Cheetie Kumar, co-owner and chef of Garland in Raleigh, North Carolina. Tighter menus help short-staffed kitchens. Add to this supply chain problems. At Maydan in Washington, D.C., owner Rose Previte says that procuring ingredients like spices and oils poses problems, in part because global distributors are facing their own labor shortages. In turn, everything is more expensive. According to Nicholas Elmi of Philadelphia's Laurel and The Landing Kitchen, "Fish went up about 10% [in June] alone." Maryland blue crab meat has more than tripled, clocking in now at nearly $55 per pound. "They don't have people to pick crab," he says. For Laurel, this means offering one tasting menu instead of two. Some chefs say scaled-down menus are not necessarily a bad thing. "Smaller menus mean more focus," chef Marcus Samuelsson says. "*Thriller* was only nine songs. This is a time when we will see American food through a different lens."

8.

Don't Weaponize Your Online Review

BY **DEPUTY EDITOR MELANIE HANSCHE**

➡ **A BAD DINING EXPERIENCE TRULY SUCKS.** I know this as both a customer and as the deputy editor of *Food & Wine*, but also as the owner of a café with my husband in Pennsylvania. You, the diner, have invested time and money to go eat delicious things that you didn't have to cook yourself, in a convivial atmosphere. When your expectations aren't met, it can be tempting to go nuclear online. And while that might make you feel vindicated in the short term, it's really not doing my restaurant–or you, honestly–any favors. What's the result, after all? You walk away feeling you've been cheated of a good night out; my business suffers in the long term from a negative online review.

Here's a better idea: If you give constructive feedback in the moment, my restaurant management can turn your subpar experience into a spectacular one because you're allowing us to practice exactly what we specialize in: hospitality. Talking to a manager and letting them know what you're not satisfied with allows us to course-correct right away. In the end, it's a win-win. You end up having a better experience (don't forget that our aim is to make you happy), and we can actually improve your day, rather than get punished in perpetuity online for a single accident or occurrence.

66% of readers say they are likely to speak to a restaurant manager if they have a bad experience.

9.

Prove Your Status

CONDENSED FROM REPORTING BY **KRISTEN HAWLEY**

➡ **WE'VE ALL MADE CONCESSIONS DURING THE PANDEMIC.** San Francisco chef Seth Stowaway figured he'd have to break up the single long table at the center of his new restaurant to space guests apart. But instead of compromising his vision for an intimate and communal dinner party, Stowaway found a simple way to safely seat strangers next to each other. When Osito opens in October, it'll join restaurants across the country in asking for proof of vaccination. Generally, restaurants are within their right to require diners to prove their vaccination status, and objecting to the vaccine–for whatever reason–isn't enough to skirt the rule. Most ask to see your vaccination card, a photo of the card, or a digital health pass. Some allow a negative COVID-19 test. Check social media accounts, read your reservation confirmation email, or just call and ask if there's a policy. Why bother? Amid surging cases, new capacity restrictions could cripple or close restaurants that have only just started to recover. Experts agree that vaccinations are among the only ways to put the pandemic behind us.

Be Kind

BY **VINNY ENG**

10.

I WAS NEW TO WAITING TABLES 15 YEARS AGO. A guest waved me over: "Can I tell you something?" I held my breath and waited. "This is exactly as you described, but it is just not for me." I first felt immediate relief, then apologized and responded in jest, "I'm always glad to set you up for gentle disappointment." We both laughed, and then we worked together to find a more suitable dish.

I thought about this experience a lot during the COVID-19 pandemic. These past 18 months demanded so much from all of us, individually and collectively. With humility and relief, and still a bit worn down, many of us have made it to the other side of the shutdown. Timeliness, candor, directness, and kindness in communication (my take on "the four gates of communication") became important tools, not only to level-set in the face of a pandemic but also to ensure that we could preserve our energies to deliver help not just to ourselves but also to the people we were riding out COVID-19 with.

I learned those communication skills working in restaurants. During the pandemic, embattled but not broken, food workers were deemed essential. They labored: at grocery stores, in dining rooms, on delivery bikes, packing takeout orders, cooking meals, and waiting tables in outdoor shared spaces–all while sustaining heightened exposure to a potentially life-ending disease.

Food workers bring dexterity, consistency, emotional intelligence, and persistence to our roles. This is skillful work, and millions of these workers ensured that other people had access to meals while still earning pre-COVID-19 wages. And because of the past 18 months, many others in the restaurant and food

As you reenter the dining world, tread softly.

industry have lost careers, emptied savings accounts, strained friendships, and ended relationships; the pandemic impoverished families and tragically caused the deaths of colleagues and loved ones. So as you reenter the dining world, with relief that your favorite spot is open again, tread softly. Pass through the four gates and recognize the humanity of every worker. Greet each employee with an acknowledgment of their presence: You are sharing space with them.

COVID-19 also revealed long-standing structural barriers to the equitable treatment of workers. Women owners, gender-fluid operators, and entrepreneurs of color all faced clear impediments that kept them from gaining access to the money they needed to stave off cash-flow crises or crushing debt. Your individual choices won't solve those burdens, but the grace you afford restaurant owners and workers may help renew their motivation to see those challenges through.

When I traveled for the first time after shelter-in-place orders were lifted, I accompanied a friend to New Orleans. We were attending a memorial that was postponed because of the pandemic. At Herbsaint, we sat at the bar and succumbed to the temptation to order one of everything. And as we settled into piping hot fried oysters and perfectly dressed coleslaw, I asked our bartender what it was like to be back in service. Unlike in San Francisco, where I live, indoor dining only paused in New Orleans for two months. But public health guidance was still hard to navigate. The bartender said he was more than pleased to be working indoors without a mask, despite the boorish behavior of some diners when mask mandates were initially lifted. The staff and rhythm of the restaurant, he said, were finally returning to pre-COVID-19 levels. He then added his plea to future diners: "Don't be an asshole."

INTRODUCING

Dewar's®

JAPANESE SMOOTH

SCOTCH WHISKY EXTRA-MATURED IN MIZUNARA OAK CASKS
FOR AN EXTRA SMOOTH & RICHER TASTE WITH NOTES OF
SANDALWOOD AND CINNAMON-LIKE SPICE

Aged **8** *Years*

HANDBOOK

Eat Like a Pro Fourteen fall-perfect recipes and pairings from our favorite chefs and somms

Angie Mar's Chicken with Roasted Grapes, Garlic, and Rosemary is a love letter to autumn.

FOOD STYLING: MARGARET MONROE DICKEY; PROP STYLING: LYDIA PURSELL

produced by JOSH MILLER   *photography by* GREG DUPREE

REDISCOVER DELICIOUS SIMPLICITY

ANGIE MAR   LES TROIS CHEVAUX, NEW YORK CITY

"I'm on record as being a slavering fan of Angie Mar's glam-bomb fare: a duck on fire, a trotter jutting up from a lard-crusted pie, a Manhattan served in a haze of smoke and a whiff of brimstone," says Senior Editor Kat Kinsman, who is a superfan of Mar, a 2017 *Food & Wine* Best New Chef. "But the takeout foil pan filled with roasted grapes, garlic, shallots, and rosemary; fatty drippings; and the sloppiest, cook's-treat parts of a chicken (my favorite) may be the best thing she ever served me. After months of my own pandemic cooking, my heart finally felt at home."

Chicken with Roasted Grapes, Garlic, and Rosemary

ACTIVE 15 MIN; TOTAL 45 MIN; SERVES 4

Dinner doesn't get simpler or more elegant than this crispy-skinned chicken. As it roasts with the juicy grapes, the chicken yields a schmaltzy pan sauce that begs for a crusty piece of bread.

- 1 (4-lb.) whole chicken, cut into 8 pieces
- 4 tsp. kosher salt
- ⅓ cup extra-virgin olive oil, divided
- 1 medium bunch red seedless grapes (about 2 cups), divided into small clusters
- 1 large garlic head, separated and cloves peeled (15 to 20 cloves)
- 1 (½-oz.) bunch fresh rosemary
- ¼ tsp. black pepper

1. Preheat oven to 400°F. Season chicken pieces with salt. Heat 1½ tablespoons oil in a large ovenproof skillet over high. Add chicken pieces, skin sides down, and cook, undisturbed, until skin is browned and crisp, about 10 minutes. Remove from heat, and transfer chicken to a plate. Add grapes, garlic cloves, and rosemary to skillet, stirring and scraping up any browned bits. Return chicken pieces to skillet, skin sides up, nestling between and atop grapes. Drizzle with remaining oil.

2. Roast in preheated oven until a meat thermometer inserted in chicken breast registers 155°F, 22 to 25 minutes. Let chicken rest 10 minutes; sprinkle with black pepper. —*ANGIE MAR, LES TROIS CHEVAUX, NEW YORK CITY*

WINE Full-bodied, fruity white: 2019 Raeburn Russian River Valley Chardonnay

▼
GO NATURAL
Seek out a best-quality bird for this simple, focused dish, such as a pastured chicken from whiteoak pastures.com.

portrait illustrations by ALEXANDRA COMPAIN-TISSIER

Thermador ★®

7 Products in One
With the Capacity to Do It All

Designed to Compromise Nothing. Including Possibilities.

 Star® Burners with ExtraLow®

Dual Zone, Double Griddle

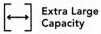 Up to 22,000 BTUs

Extra Large Capacity

Learn more at **THERMADOR.COM/RANGES**

PAT THE CAKES
Be sure to drain the
tofu and pat it dry thor-
oughly before cooking
so it absorbs all the
toasty spices.

photography by VICTOR PROTASIO

REIMAGINE THE FLAVORS OF THE PAST

JOCELYN LAW-YONE   THAMEE, WASHINGTON, D.C.

"MY GRANDPARENTS, who were from different parts of the world, colored my flavor map," says Jocelyn Law-Yone, executive chef and co-owner of Thamee in Washington, D.C., a 2020 *Food & Wine* Best New Restaurant. "My paternal grandfather was from Yunnan, China, where tofu is enjoyed in countless ways by many different tribes. In Burma, where both my grandmothers were born, there's a counterpart of tofu called 'tohu'–it mimics the texture of tofu but tastes nuttier because it is made of besan flour." Known as "Chef JoJo" to her team, Law-Yone combined elements from her grandparents' cooking with her own twists to create her namesake version of mapo tofu, a traditional Szechuan dish. "The additional layers of mushrooms and eggplants are mine but would have been familiar ingredients to all my grandparents."

MaJo Tofu

TOTAL 50 MIN; SERVES 4

Finely chopped eggplant and mushrooms cook down to a meaty consistency that absorbs a richly savory blend of broad bean paste and mushroom seasoning, two umami-packed ingredients that quickly add long-cooked flavor. Szechuan peppercorns and piquant fresh ginger are balanced by a touch of sugar to round out this moderately spicy dish.

1   **cup hot water**

1   **tsp. mushroom seasoning (such as Po Lo Ku)**

6 to 8 **dried red chiles, seeded and roughly chopped (about 1½ Tbsp.)**

½   **cup neutral oil (such as canola or grapeseed), divided**

2   **tsp. Szechuan peppercorns, finely ground, plus more for garnish**

3   **Tbsp. finely chopped yellow onion**

2   **Tbsp. finely chopped peeled fresh ginger**

2   **Tbsp. finely chopped garlic**

1½ **cups finely chopped (about ¼-inch pieces) Japanese eggplant**

5   **oz. finely chopped button mushrooms (about 1¾ cups)**

3   **Tbsp. broad bean paste with red chile oil (such as Sichuan Pixian)**

1   **lb. firm tofu, drained, patted dry, and cut into ¾- to 1-inch pieces**

¾   **cup thinly sliced scallions, divided**

1   **Tbsp. soy sauce**

1   **tsp. granulated sugar**

¼   **tsp. toasted sesame oil**

1. Stir together 1 cup hot water and mushroom seasoning in a small bowl until well dissolved. Set aside.

2. Toast chiles in a 14-inch wok over medium-low, stirring often, until fragrant, about 1 minute. Add ¼ cup neutral oil, and cook, stirring often, until chiles turn a rust color, 1 to 2 minutes. (Do not burn chiles.) Transfer mixture to a small bowl; set aside.

3. Heat remaining ¼ cup neutral oil in wok over medium. Add ground Szechuan peppercorns, and cook, stirring constantly, until fragrant, about 30 seconds. Add onion, ginger, and garlic. Cook, stirring often, until softened, about 2 minutes. Increase heat to high, and add eggplant and mushrooms. Cook, stirring often, until very tender, 5 to 7 minutes. Stir in broad bean paste until well combined. Stir in reserved mushroom seasoning mixture. Cook, stirring occasionally, until mixture has reduced to a thick paste, 5 to 8 minutes.

4. Stir in tofu and chile-oil mixture. Cook, stirring often, until mixture has thickened slightly, 2 to 4 minutes. Stir in ¼ cup scallions, soy sauce, sugar, and sesame oil. Cook, stirring often, until scallions are wilted, about 2 minutes. Top with remaining ½ cup scallions, and garnish with ground Szechaun peppercorns. —*JOCELYN LAW-YONE, THAMEE, WASHINGTON, D.C.*

WINE Richer-style rosé: 2020 Cune Rosado

NOTE Find mushroom seasoning, broad bean paste, and Szechuan peppercorns at Asian grocery stores or online at asiafoodusa.com and justasianfood.com.

COZY UP TO CHICKEN AND RICE

GEORGE MENDES   VERANDA, NEW YORK CITY

"**MY PARENTS WERE PORTUGUESE IMMIGRANTS,** so I grew up with my mom cooking many rice dishes for my family," says 2011 *Food & Wine* Best New Chef George Mendes, who opened Veranda in New York last spring. "There was simple tomato rice served with fried fish and then rabbit rice on special occasions and holidays. Through my career, I always let these memories inspire me, hence the duck rice at my previous restaurant, Aldea, and then at home recently with this chicken dish."

Arroz de Galinha (Portuguese Chicken and Rice)

ACTIVE 25 MIN; TOTAL 1 HR; SERVES 4

Crispy bits of chicken, crunchy rice, and briny olive slices come together for the perfect bite in this effortless, comforting chicken-and-rice dinner, perfumed with heady saffron.

- 1½   cups lower-sodium chicken broth or vegetable broth
- 1   cup uncooked white basmati rice (not rinsed)
- ¼   tsp. plus 1 pinch of kosher salt, divided
- 20   saffron threads (scant ¼ tsp.)
- ⅛   tsp. black pepper
- 2   Tbsp. olive oil
- 1   small yellow onion, finely chopped (about 1 cup)
- 3   garlic cloves, minced
- ½   cup finely chopped red bell pepper
- 3   oz. soppressata, peeled and sliced into half-moons (about ½ cup)
- 1   (about 2-lb.) whole rotisserie chicken, skin discarded, meat picked and shredded (3 to 4 cups)
- ¼   cup pitted kalamata olives, sliced

1. Bring broth to a simmer in a medium saucepan over medium. Stir in rice, ¼ teaspoon salt, saffron, and pepper. Cover and reduce heat to low; cook, undisturbed, 20 minutes. Remove from heat. Let stand, covered, 5 to 10 minutes. Uncover and fluff with a fork. Set aside.

2. Preheat oven to 400°F. Heat oil in a large ovenproof skillet over medium. Add onion, garlic, and remaining pinch of salt; cook, stirring often, until onion is light golden, about 5 minutes. Add bell pepper; cook, stirring often, 5 minutes. Add soppressata; stir well to combine. Cook, stirring often, until soppressata begins to render, about 5 minutes. Remove from heat; stir in chicken and olives. Top with cooked rice. Carefully stir mixture to combine, and flatten slightly using a spatula.

3. Bake in preheated oven 8 minutes. Stir mixture using a fork. Continue baking until rice is slightly crisped on top and around sides, about 3 minutes. Serve family-style. —*GEORGE MENDES, VERANDA, NEW YORK CITY*

WINE Robust, peppery Portuguese red: 2016 Herdade do Esporão Reserva

TASTES LIKE
A SUNSET BY THE SEA.

TASTES LIKE **PUERTO RICO.**

Here, our cuisine is more than just local ingredients and traditions. It's more than international influences and incredible variety. It's all of that, plus the indescribable essence of everything else that makes this Island so unique. It's the distinct passion flowing through the veins of our people that infuses each dish and each drink with a flavor you can't find anywhere else. Learn more at **DiscoverPuertoRico.com.**

DISCOVER
Puerto Rico

CHOOSE YOUR ANCHOVY ADVENTURE

STUART BRIOZA   THE ANCHOVY BAR, SAN FRANCISCO

THE ANCHOVY BAR, SISTER RESTAURANT to State Bird Provisions in San Francisco, celebrates the tiny, humble fish in a host of ways, including this made-to-share snack board. "The build-your-own aspect of this dish makes the simplicity work so well," says co-owner Nicole Krasinski, who opened the restaurant with her husband, Stuart Brioza, a 2003 *Food & Wine* Best New Chef. "Everything is meant to be clean and fresh and offer a great balance to the salty anchovies."

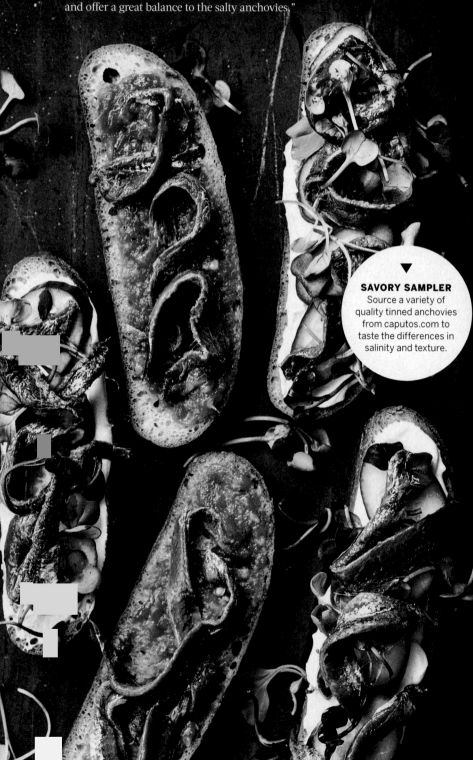

▼

SAVORY SAMPLER
Source a variety of quality tinned anchovies from caputos.com to taste the differences in salinity and texture.

Anchovy Toasts with Fresh Tomato Vinaigrette

ACTIVE 20 MIN; TOTAL 45 MIN
SERVES 4 TO 6

Quality Spanish anchovy fillets, ripe heirloom tomatoes, and fresh Japanese cucumbers shine in this build-your-own toast board that's ideal for entertaining or a light alfresco meal. Try leftover tomato vinaigrette tossed with pasta as a simple no-cook sauce.

TOMATO VINAIGRETTE

- 1 lb. ripe heirloom tomatoes, stemmed and halved
- ¼ cup extra-virgin olive oil
- ½ tsp. kosher salt, plus more to taste
- ⅛ tsp. black pepper, plus more to taste

ADDITIONAL INGREDIENTS

- 8 (½-inch-thick) ciabatta slices (about 1½ oz. each)
- ¼ cup extra-virgin olive oil
- 1 large garlic clove
- 1 (1.7-oz.) can olive oil–packed salted anchovy fillets (such as Don Bocarte, Callol Serrats, or Delfino Battista) (6 to 7 fillets)
- ½ cup crème fraîche
- 1 medium-size Japanese cucumber, thinly sliced (about 1¼ cups)
- ¼ cup radish sprouts (about ½ oz.)

1. Make the tomato vinaigrette: Grate cut sides of tomatoes on large holes of a box grater set over a medium bowl until only tomato skin and core remain; discard skin and core. Whisk oil, salt, and pepper into grated tomato until well combined. Season with additional salt and pepper to taste, if desired. Set aside.

2. Make the anchovy toasts: Preheat oven to 400°F. Brush both sides of ciabatta slices evenly with oil, and arrange in a single layer on a rimmed baking sheet. Bake in preheated oven until lightly toasted, 8 to 12 minutes. Let cool on baking sheet 5 minutes. Lightly rub garlic clove over top side of each toast, about 2 swipes per slice.

3. Arrange anchovies on a small plate. Serve alongside toasts, crème fraîche, cucumber, radish sprouts, and ½ cup vinaigrette. Reserve remaining vinaigrette for another use. Assemble as desired.
—STUART BRIOZA, THE ANCHOVY BAR, SAN FRANCISCO

MAKE AHEAD Tomato vinaigrette can be stored in an airtight container in refrigerator up to 2 days. Let come to room temperature and stir well before serving.

WINE Crisp, lightly tingly Txakoli: 2020 Txomin Etxaniz

Flex your antioxidant muscles.

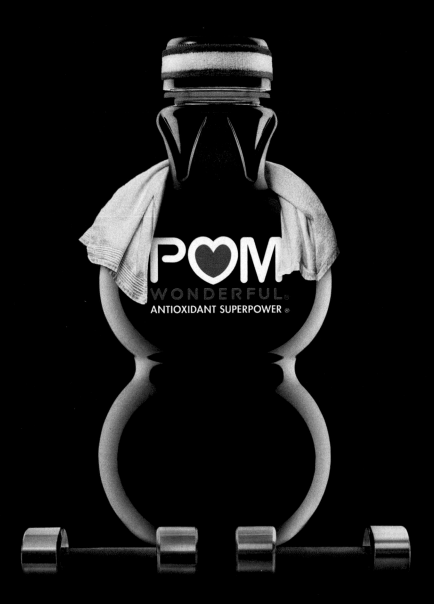

The Antioxidant Superpower, POM Wonderful, has 700 mg of polyphenol antioxidants in every 8oz bottle. Making it the perfect workout partner the next time you hit the gym.

LAMB HOTPOT

Discover the authentic taste of modern Irish cuisine with this original recipe from JP McMahon and Kerrygold.

Preparation: 30 minutes
Cooking: 1 hour 10 minutes
Serves 6–8

INGREDIENTS

- 1.5 pounds lamb shoulder, diced
- 3 onions, sliced
- 2 tablespoons finely chopped thyme
- 2 tablespoons plain (all-purpose) flour
- 3 cups lamb stock warmed
- 1.5 pounds (7 medium) potatoes, peeled and thinly sliced
- 7 tablespoons Kerrygold Pure Irish Butter
- Rapeseed oil, for frying
- Sea salt and freshly ground black pepper

HOW TO MAKE IT

1. Preheat the oven to 350°F.

2. Season the lamb with black pepper and salt.

3. Heat 3.5 tablespoons of butter with a little oil in a cast iron pot over a medium heat, add the lamb and fry, in batches, for 5-10 minutes until nicely browned. Remove and reserve in a warm place.

4. Add the onions and half the thyme to the pot and cook for about 5 minutes until soft and translucent. To make a roux, add the flour and cook for 2 minutes to form a loose paste. Gradually pour in the warm lamb stock and stir until the roux has dissolved.

5. Return the browned lamb to the pot. Place the potato slices on top in a circular pattern. Melt the remaining butter. Brush with the melted butter and season with sea salt, black pepper, and the remaining thyme.

6. Cover and bake in the preheated oven for 45 minutes. Remove the lid during the last 15 minutes to allow the potatoes to brown.

RECIPE BY JP MCMAHON, ADAPTED FROM THE IRISH COOKBOOK (PHAIDON 2020). SIGNED COPIES AVAILABLE TO PURCHASE: FROM HTTPS://WWW.ANIARRESTAURANT.IE/THE-IRISH-COOKBOOK.

Ireland's Food Ambassador: JP McMahon

In the charming city of Galway, on Ireland's rugged west coast, Chef JP McMahon is quietly changing the way the world thinks about modern Irish cuisine.

THE TINY ISLAND NATION of Ireland has a food culture that dates back 10,000 years; it's a rich and storied past that Chef JP McMahon, along with Kerrygold, are determined to share with food-lovers around the globe.

THE LAND

Growing up in Ireland, among farmers, has profoundly influenced the way McMahon thinks about food and cooking. "The size of Ireland is important. It's small," he says. "We still have a very strong connection with the land." This connection has led McMahon to build his menus around locally produced ingredients. "You get a product and then you make a dish, not the

other way around," he says. McMahon considers Kerrygold's butter and cheese, made with milk from Irish grass-fed cows, to be ideal ingredient staples.

THE CUISINE

"Irish food is about oysters and seaweed just as much as it's about potatoes and lamb stew," explains McMahon, adding that Ireland's produce is some of the best in the world. So when McMahon opened his now Michelin-starred Aniar 10-plus years ago, he committed to using only ingredients produced on the island: wild herbs, wildflowers, seafood, and—yes—seaweed. It's a unique concept that has earned the restaurant the attention of food lovers around the world.

To learn more about Kerrygold butter and cheeses, visit **kerrygoldusa.com**.

DAILY GRIND
For the brightest flavor, toast and grind whole spices in small batches just before adding to this curry or any dish.

CELEBRATE HUMBLE BEGINNINGS

MARGARET PAK   THATTU, CHICAGO

"**GOING THROUGH PHOTOS RECENTLY,** I discovered that 2003 was my first time tasting egg curry," says chef Margaret Pak of Thattu in Chicago, a 2020 *Food & Wine* Best New Restaurant. "My boyfriend (now husband) made it for me (along with crab curry, eggplant, and a couple other dishes). I was mesmerized that a simple egg dish could be so comforting and delicious. It makes me so happy to know that this humble recipe is what planted the seed to open Thattu."

Keralan Egg Curry

TOTAL 45 MIN; SERVES 4 TO 6

Coconut milk, tomatoes, and onions add vegetal sweetness that rounds out the fruity piquancy of Kashmiri chile powder and Thai chiles in this warmly spiced curry. Curry sprigs are tender and will continue to add flavor after cooking; feel free to leave them in for serving.

5 tsp. coriander seeds

4 tsp. fennel seeds

2 tsp. ground turmeric

2 tsp. Kashmiri chile powder or smoked paprika

¼ cup canola oil

2 Tbsp. finely chopped peeled fresh ginger

4 medium garlic cloves, finely chopped (about 2 tsp.)

4 to 6 fresh green Thai chiles, split lengthwise with stem ends left intact, seeds removed

2 (8-inch) curry sprigs

2 medium-size red onions (about 1½ lb.), chopped (about 4 cups)

4 medium-size plum tomatoes (about 14 oz.), cored and finely chopped (about 2 cups)

½ cup water, plus more as needed

2 tsp. kosher salt, plus more to taste

6 hard-cooked eggs, peeled and halved lengthwise

2 (13.5-oz.) cans unsweetened coconut milk, shaken and stirred

Fresh cilantro, for garnish

Cooked basmati rice, for serving

1. Toast coriander and fennel seeds in a small skillet over medium-low, stirring often, until fragrant, about 3 minutes. Remove from skillet, and let cool 5 minutes. Using a spice grinder or a mortar and pestle, grind coriander and fennel seeds until a fine powder forms. Transfer to a small bowl; add turmeric and chile powder, and set aside.

2. Heat oil in a large saucepan over medium. Add ginger, garlic, Thai chiles, and curry sprigs; cook, stirring constantly, until fragrant, about 20 seconds. Add onions; cook, stirring occasionally, until softened, 10 to 14 minutes. Stir in coriander mixture; cook, stirring constantly, until fragrant, about 1 minute. Add tomatoes, ½ cup water, and salt; cook, stirring often and scraping bottom of pan, until tomatoes begin to break down and mixture forms a coarse paste, about 5 minutes.

3. Add eggs, cut sides up, to mixture in pan. Pour in coconut milk, and gently stir to combine. Reduce heat to medium-low; cook, stirring occasionally, until flavors meld and eggs are heated through, about 10 minutes. Add additional water, 2 tablespoons at a time, if a thinner consistency is desired. Season with additional salt to taste. Garnish with cilantro. Serve with basmati rice.
—*MARGARET PAK, THATTU, CHICAGO*

WINE Lemony, earthy, firmly acidic white: Domaine de l'Ecu Granite Muscadet

NOTE Find Kashmiri chile powder, fresh Thai chiles, and curry leaves at South Asian grocery stores or online at subziwalla.com.

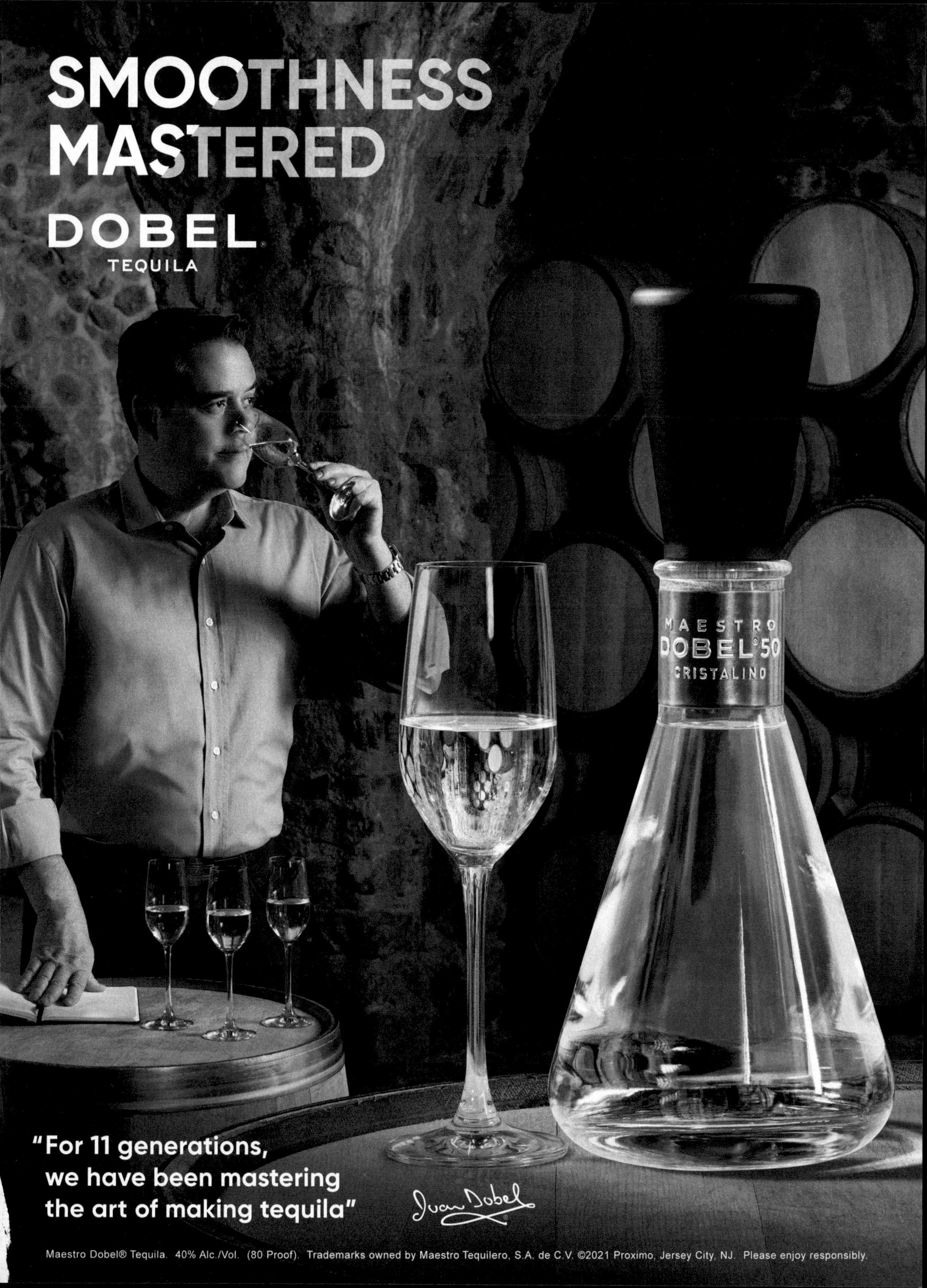
SMOOTHNESS
MASTERED
DOBEL
TEQUILA
MAESTRO
DOBEL 50
CRISTALINO
"For 11 generations,
we have been mastering
the art of making tequila"
Juan Dobel
Maestro Dobel® Tequila. 40% Alc./Vol. (80 Proof). Trademarks owned by Maestro Tequilero, S.A. de C.V. ©2021 Proximo, Jersey City, NJ. Please enjoy responsibly.

▼

A GRATE IDEA
No potato ricer?
No problem. Grate the
cooled potatoes on the
small holes of a box
grater for a similar
texture.

1. Preheat oven to 350°F. Place potatoes directly on middle rack of preheated oven, and bake until tender, about 1 hour and 15 minutes. Remove from oven. Carefully cut potatoes in half lengthwise; let stand until cool enough to handle, about 20 minutes. Scoop potato flesh into a ricer; discard skins. Process potatoes through ricer into a large bowl. Add, but do not stir in, cheese, egg yolks, 1½ teaspoons salt, and pepper. Sprinkle flour over mixture; using your hands, fold together until well incorporated and mixture forms a soft dough ball, about 1 minute. Wrap dough with plastic wrap; refrigerate 30 minutes. Remove dough from refrigerator, and unwrap. Place dough on a floured work surface, and cut dough evenly into 5 pieces. Using your hands, roll each piece into a 12½-inch-long rope. Cut each rope into 1-inch pieces. Roll each piece until it is about 1½ inches long. Place on a lightly floured baking sheet lined with parchment paper.

2. Bring 16 cups water and ¼ cup salt to a boil in a large Dutch oven over high. Fill a large bowl with ice water. Add gnocchi to boiling water; cook, stirring occasionally, until gnocchi begin to float, about 2 minutes. Transfer to ice water; let cool 3 minutes. Drain well. Transfer gnocchi to a large bowl; add oil, and toss gently. Cover and refrigerate up to 3 hours.

3. Process tomatoes in a blender until smooth, about 10 seconds. Transfer tomato puree to a large saucepan; add basil, garlic, and sugar. Bring to a simmer over medium-low. Simmer, stirring occasionally, until thickened, about 45 minutes. Add butter and remaining ½ teaspoon salt; stir until butter melts.

4. Place gnocchi in tomato sauce; simmer over medium-low, stirring occasionally, until warmed, about 5 minutes. Garnish servings with additional cheese and basil, if desired. —*ERIC LEES*

MAKE AHEAD Gnocchi can be prepared through step 1 and placed in freezer until frozen. Transfer to ziplock plastic freezer bags, and freeze up to 6 weeks. Continue with blanching and cooking in tomato sauce as directed.

WINE Vibrant, complex Tuscan Red: 2015 Casanova di Neri Brunello di Montalcino

SAVOR THE PERFECT PAIRING

ERIC LEES   SPIAGGIA, CHICAGO

"**I ABSOLUTELY LOVE THIS DISH** and could eat it every day," says Rachael Lowe, former beverage director of Chicago's Spiaggia and a 2016 *Food & Wine* Sommelier of the Year. "I love to drink the Piombaia Brunello di Montalcino 2015 with it; on the palate, the integrated-yet-present acidity balances out the racy tomato sauce, while the slightly grippy tannins cut through the richness of the gnocchi." Sadly the restaurant closed last summer; hopefully this recipe from chef Eric Lees will provide a taste of the joy Spiaggia served over its 37-year history.

Gnocchi with Pomodoro Sauce

ACTIVE 1 HR 30 MIN; TOTAL 3 HR 35 MIN
SERVES 4 TO 6

Tender gnocchi, with a delicate bite from starchy russet potatoes, get a pleasant rich-ness from nutty Parmigiano-Reggiano and silky egg yolks incorporated into the dough. Easy to make and freeze ahead of time, the pasta finishes by gently simmering in a but-tery tomato sauce laced with fresh basil.

1¼ lb. russet potatoes (about 2 small potatoes)

1½ oz. Parmigiano-Reggiano cheese, grated using a Microplane grater (about 1 cup), plus more for garnish

2 large egg yolks

¼ cup plus 2 tsp. kosher salt, divided

½ tsp. cracked black pepper

¾ cup 00 flour (about 3 oz.) or ¾ cup all-purpose flour (about 3¼ oz.), plus more for work surface

16 cups water

1 tsp. canola oil

1 (28-oz.) can whole peeled San Marzano plum tomatoes

2 Tbsp. chopped fresh basil, plus more for garnish

1 Tbsp. finely chopped garlic

2 tsp. granulated sugar

6 Tbsp. unsalted butter (3 oz.)

DISCOVER
South Carolina

SC *is* OPEN

Myrtle Beach, South Carolina

Whether you're spending Thanksgiving along the Grand Strand or enjoying the wide, white sand beaches and oceanfront eateries in Myrtle Beach, South Carolina is the perfect fall destination. Discover a cooler kind of summer at FALLinSC.com

SC *is* OPEN

Myrtle Beach, South Carolina

Get to Know Yondu

Crafted from fermented soybeans and a variety of vegetables, a few drops of Yondu bring out the depth and complexity of your favorite plant-based dishes at any stage of the cooking process.

THE FLAVOR AND versatility of Yondu makes it the perfect accompaniment for all kinds of recipes — from soups to sauces and dips to stir-fries.

HERE ARE A FEW WAYS TO USE YONDU TO TRANSFORM SOME MEALTIME FAVORITES:

FALL PASTA

With Yondu in the pantry, you're only minutes away from a pasta that enhances the naturally sweet and savory flavors of seasonal autumn staples. In the same pan, toss roasted squash, Tuscan kale, red cabbage, and yellow onions with Yondu, then combine with al dente rigatoni for a simple but flavorful dinner.

3-MINUTE VEGETABLE SOUP

Create an effortlessly rich seasonal broth with your favorite fall vegetables by simply adding Yondu. Combine three cups of water with one cup of assorted, diced vegetables. Simmer for three minutes before stirring in one tablespoon of Yondu.

YONDU FRIED RICE

You won't need multiple sauces and seasonings to flavor your fried rice, just two tablespoons of Yondu. Simply sauté your preferred vegetables like shiitake mushrooms, carrots, or snow peas with one tablespoon of Yondu. Add two cups of cooked rice, mix your ingredients, then add the second tablespoon of Yondu.

vegetable umami

Yondu®

VISIT YONDU.US/RECIPES AND DISCOVER EVEN MORE WAYS TO USE THIS STAPLE TO ADD A RICH LAYER OF FLAVOR TO YOUR FAVORITE DISHES!

Need an Easy, Plant-Based Flavor Boost?

Expand your arsenal of go-to recipes with Yondu umami seasoning sauce as your plant-based shortcut to flavor; it will quickly become a pantry staple for whenever you want to add deep, rich flavor to any dish.

vegetable
umami
Yondu®

gluten free   gmo free   organic

vegan   no msg

FILL, FOLD, FRY ...
DIP, EAT, REPEAT

KIKI ARANITA   PHILADELPHIA

"AT THE MANY Hawaiian family feasts that I attend, gau gee are ubiquitous," says Kiki Aranita, a Philadelphia-based chef. "I'm also half Chinese, so this recipe uses the pork-and-chestnut filling that I learned to make as a child in Hong Kong. Wontons are the one thing that we always made at home and wrangled everyone available to help fold."

SPICY MAYO DIP
Stir together ½ cup mayonnaise and ½ teaspoon Poi Dog Chili Peppah Water or ichimi togarashi.

Crispy Pork–and–Water Chestnut Gau Gee

ACTIVE 45 MIN; TOTAL 3 HR; SERVES 6 TO 8

Toasted sesame oil and crunchy water chestnuts enrich the pork filling in these fried wontons. For the dipping sauce, seek out Aranita's version of chile pepper water, a staple Hawaiian condiment.

- 8   oz. ground pork
- ½   cup roughly chopped water chestnuts
- 2   Tbsp. soy sauce
- 2   Tbsp. thinly sliced scallion
- 1   Tbsp. toasted sesame oil
- 2¼ tsp. granulated sugar
- 1   tsp. finely chopped peeled fresh ginger
- ½   tsp. finely chopped garlic
- ¼   tsp. kosher salt
- 1   large egg
- 1½ Tbsp. water
- ¼   cup cornstarch
- 40 yellow egg wonton wrappers
     Canola oil, for frying
     Spicy Mayo Dip (recipe above)

1. Combine ground pork, water chestnuts, soy sauce, scallion, sesame oil, sugar, ginger, garlic, and salt in a large bowl; mix thoroughly with your hands until just combined. Cover and refrigerate 2 to 12 hours.

2. Line a large rimmed baking sheet with parchment paper. Whisk together egg and 1½ tablespoons water in a small bowl. Place cornstarch in a shallow bowl. Working with 1 wonton wrapper at a time, place about 1 teaspoon pork filling on center of wrapper. Using a finger, trace 2 connected edges of the wrapper with some of the egg wash; fold the wrapper in half to form a triangle, pressing gently on filling to eliminate air pockets. Dust bottom of gau gee lightly with some of the cornstarch to prevent sticking; place on prepared baking sheet. Repeat process with remaining wrappers and filling. Cover and freeze at least 15 minutes.

3. Pour canola oil into a large Dutch oven to a depth of 1½ inches. Heat over medium-high until a deep-fry thermometer registers 375°F. Working in 6 or 7 batches, add 6 gau gee to hot oil; fry, stirring occasionally, until golden brown, 1 minute and 30 seconds to 2 minutes. Drain gau gee on a plate lined with paper towels. Serve warm with spicy mayo dip.
—*KIKI ARANITA, PHILADELPHIA*

MAKE AHEAD Assembled gau gee can be frozen up to 2 months.

WINE Lively, aromatic Pinot Grigio: 2019 Peter Zemmer Alto Adige

NOTE Find Poi Dog Chili Peppah Water seasoning at poidogphilly.com.

NO EXTRA STUFF

Adding herbs to your dish may be delicious, but extra stuff in tea isn't.
So we say no to artificial flavors and yes to the finest ingredients, expertly crafted.

NO ARTIFICIAL SWEETENERS. NO ARTIFICIAL FLAVORS. NO IS *beautiful.*

MAKE THE SALSA THAT BRINGS FOLKS BACK

EDGAR RICO NIXTA TAQUERIA, AUSTIN

"**BEFORE WE OPENED OUR RESTAURANT,** my husband, Edgar, and I were newly self-employed and looking for ways to stay afloat," says Sara Mardanbigi, co-owner of Nixta Taqueria, in Austin, a 2020 *Food & Wine* Best New Restaurant. "We started hustling Airbnb Experiences at our house with cooking classes. One of the most popular items guests raved about was the romesco salsa. Once Nixta opened, we ran the cauliflower taco topped with it as a seasonal option, and then, because it was in such high demand, we made it a menu staple. To this day, we'll get Airbnb guests coming by to see our taqueria baby in real life—and to try the cauliflower taco, of course!"

Charred Cauliflower Tacos with Romesco Salsa

ACTIVE 30 MIN; TOTAL 1 HR 20 MIN SERVES 4

A smoky, mildly spicy romesco salsa seeps into charred cauliflower florets in this well-balanced vegetarian taco. Pine nuts add crunch and richness to each bite.

ROMESCO SALSA

- 3 medium-size red bell peppers
- 1 (3½-oz.) plum tomato
- ¾ cup toasted pecan halves
- ½ bunch fresh cilantro
- 3 large garlic cloves
- 3 Tbsp. fresh lemon juice
- 2 Tbsp. red wine vinegar
- 1 Tbsp. smoked paprika
- ½ tsp. cayenne pepper
- ½ cup extra-virgin olive oil
- 1 Tbsp. kosher salt

TACOS

- 1 medium head cauliflower, cut into 1½-inch florets (about 6 cups)
- ¼ cup canola oil
- 12 (6-inch) blue corn tortillas, warmed
- 4 oz. queso fresco, crumbled (about 1 cup)
- 1 cup loosely packed fresh cilantro leaves
- 2 Tbsp. toasted pine nuts
- 1 Tbsp. cold-pressed extra-virgin olive oil
   Flaky sea salt (such as Maldon), for sprinkling
- 1 lime, cut into wedges

1. Make the romesco salsa: Preheat oven to broil with oven rack about 6 inches from heat. Place bell peppers and tomato on a large rimmed baking sheet. Broil, turning twice, until charred on all sides, 10 to 15 minutes. Transfer charred peppers to a bowl, and cover with plastic wrap; let stand 30 minutes. Remove skin from tomato; quarter tomato. Remove skin, seeds, and stem from bell peppers. Process bell peppers, tomato, pecans, cilantro, garlic, lemon juice, vinegar, smoked paprika, and cayenne in a blender until smooth, about 2 minutes. With blender running on low speed, gradually add oil; process until smooth, about 30 seconds. Stir in salt.

2. Make the tacos: Preheat oven to high broil with oven rack about 6 inches from heat. Toss together cauliflower florets and canola oil on a large rimmed baking sheet. Broil, stirring twice, until cauliflower is browned, 10 to 15 minutes.

3. Top each tortilla with about ¼ cup roasted cauliflower, 2 tablespoons romesco salsa, and 1 tablespoon queso fresco. Garnish with cilantro and pine nuts, and finish with olive oil, a sprinkle of flaky sea salt, and a squeeze of lime juice. —*EDGAR RICO, NIXTA TAQUERIA, AUSTIN*

MAKE AHEAD Romesco can be made up to 5 days ahead and stored in an airtight container in refrigerator.

BEER Mexican pilsner: Modelo Especial

FOOD STYLING: MARGARET MONROE DICKEY; PROP STYLING: LYDIA PURSELL

photography by GREG DUPREE

NEW

MADE IN ITALY.
Authentically delicious.

Discover more

Crafted with tomatoes vine ripened
under the Italian sun, finely aged Italian cheeses,
fresh cream and Mediterranean olive oil.

SMART SHORTCUTS
While the chefs always use fresh lobster, precooked lobster and store-bought stock make this dish weeknight-friendly.

▼

CREATE CLAWS FOR APPLAUSE

ANDREW TAYLOR AND MIKE WILEY   EVENTIDE OYSTER CO., PORTLAND, ME

"**LOBSTER STEW IS** one of the pillars of Maine cooking," according to chefs Mike Wiley and Andrew Taylor, of Eventide Oyster Co. in Portland. "We took cues from tom kha, the coconut milk–based Thai soup, and enriched it with umami-heavy Golden Mountain sauce and hen-of-the-woods mushroom confit to create this decadent stew."

Green Curry Lobster Stew

ACTIVE 25 MIN; TOTAL 1 HR 10 MIN
SERVES 4 TO 6

Sweet potato, curry paste, heavy cream, and coconut milk come together in a richly aromatic and well-balanced broth that highlights the sweetness of lobster. Chefs Taylor and Wiley cleverly use sweet potato peels to thicken the broth; they lend a creamy, pleasantly thick body to the stew.

- 8   cups boiling water
- 2½ Tbsp. lobster stock base (such as Better Than Bouillon)
- ¼   cup neutral oil (such as canola or grapeseed), divided
- ¼   cup green curry paste (such as Maesri)
- 2   oz. palm sugar, roughly chopped (about ¼ cup)
- 2   Tbsp. fish sauce
- 1   Tbsp. fermented soybean seasoning sauce (such as Golden Mountain)
- 1   large (about 1¼-lb.) sweet potato, washed, peeled (skins reserved), and flesh cut into ¾-inch cubes (about 3¾ cups), divided

      Kosher salt, to taste
- 1   lb. hen-of-the-woods mushrooms, trimmed and separated into small clusters (about 5 cups)
- ½   cup heavy cream
- ½   cup well-shaken and stirred unsweetened coconut milk
- 8   oz. cooked and picked lobster meat (such as Luke's Lobster), roughly chopped (about 1½ cups)

      Chile oil (such as La-Yu), for garnish

1. Stir together 8 cups boiling water and lobster stock base in a 2-quart measuring cup until fully dissolved; set aside. Heat 2 tablespoons oil in a medium Dutch oven over medium. Add curry paste; cook, stirring constantly, until fragrant, about 2 minutes. Add stock mixture, palm sugar, fish sauce, seasoning sauce, and sweet potato skins. Bring to a boil over medium-high. Reduce heat to medium-low, and cook, uncovered, stirring occasionally, until sweet potato skins are tender, about 15 minutes.

2. Transfer curry mixture to a blender (in batches, if needed). Secure lid on blender, and remove center piece of blender lid. Cover opening with a kitchen towel, and process until smooth, 30 seconds to 1 minute. Stir in salt to taste. Set aside.

3. Wipe Dutch oven clean. Heat remaining 2 tablespoons oil over medium. Add mushrooms, and cook, stirring occasionally, until tender, 6 to 8 minutes. Stir in curry mixture, heavy cream, coconut milk, and cubed sweet potato. Bring to a boil over medium-high. Reduce heat to medium-low, and cook, uncovered, stirring occasionally, until sweet potato is tender, 15 to 20 minutes. Remove from heat, and stir in lobster meat. Let stand until warmed through, about 2 minutes. Season with salt to taste. Garnish with chile oil. —*ANDREW TAYLOR AND MIKE WILEY, EVENTIDE OYSTER CO., PORTLAND, MAINE*

BEER Citrusy, crisp, hazy IPA: Ecliptic Brewing Phaser Hazy IPA

NOTE Find green curry paste and fermented soybean seasoning sauce at South Asian grocery stores or online at thaigrocer.com.

Smoked Ham Hock–and–Lentil Soup

ACTIVE 45 MIN; TOTAL 3 HR; SERVES 6

To make your own croutons for this rich, brothy soup, toss 3 cups of cubed baguette with 3 tablespoons butter and ¼ teaspoon kosher salt; bake at 375°F, stirring three times, until toasted, about 15 minutes.

- 2 (10-oz.) smoked ham hocks
- 3 qt. plus 3 cups water, divided
- 1 Tbsp. olive oil, plus more for drizzling
- 1 cup finely chopped Spanish onion
- 1 cup sliced okra (⅛-inch-thick slices)
- 1 (½-oz.) lemongrass stalk, finely chopped (about 2 Tbsp.)
- 1 small fresh habanero chile, finely chopped (about 1 Tbsp.)
- 1 Tbsp. finely chopped peeled fresh ginger
- 2 tsp. kosher salt, plus more to taste
- 2 cups uncooked dried red or yellow lentils
- ½ cup thinly sliced scallions
- 1½ tsp. chopped fresh thyme, plus thyme leaves, for garnish

  Microgreens and croutons, for serving

1. Bring ham hocks and 3 quarts water to a boil in a large stockpot over high. Reduce heat to low to maintain a gentle boil; partially cover, and cook, undisturbed, until meat is tender, about 2 hours. Remove hocks; remove and discard skin from hocks. Remove meat from bones, and roughly chop; set aside. Skim and discard fat from surface of stock. Set stock aside.

2. Heat oil in a large stockpot over medium. Add onion, okra, lemongrass, habanero, and ginger; cook, stirring often, until onion is translucent, 4 to 6 minutes. Stir in salt. Add lentils, remaining 3 cups water, and 3 cups reserved stock; bring to a boil over medium-high, stirring occasionally. Reduce heat to medium, and cook, stirring occasionally, until lentils are tender, 7 to 14 minutes, adding additional stock to thin, if needed. Remove 1 cup soup, and place in blender. Secure lid on blender, and remove center piece from lid. Cover opening with a kitchen towel. Process until smooth, about 20 seconds. Stir into soup. Stir in scallions, chopped thyme, and reserved chopped ham. Season with additional salt to taste. Top servings with oil, thyme leaves, microgreens, and croutons. —*NINA COMPTON, COMPÈRE LAPIN, NEW ORLEANS*

MAKE AHEAD Stock can be frozen up to 1 month.

WINE Bacony, rich California Syrah: 2019 Tensley Santa Barbara County

ROCK THIS STOCK

NINA COMPTON   COMPÈRE LAPIN, NEW ORLEANS

"I LOVE MAKING THIS SOUP when the weather begins to cool," says 2017 *Food & Wine* Best New Chef Nina Compton, chef-owner of New Orleans hot spot Compère Lapin. "The ham-hock aroma hangs around the kitchen beautifully; the smell alone makes you warmer. Adding a little ginger and lemongrass brightens the soup and reminds me of being back home in St. Lucia. Using local okra reminds me of my Louisiana home and adds a different texture."

the desert is

HOT

EAT THE STREETS' BEST TREATS

TOM PISHA-DUFFLY   GADO GADO, PORTLAND, OR

"THE FIRST THING I think about when I dream of my visits to Indonesia are *kaki lima,* the multicolored carts selling noodles, snacks, and very often bakso," says chef Tom Pisha-Duffly of Gado Gado in Portland, Oregon, one of *Food & Wine*'s Best New Restaurants in 2020. "The loud signs painted on the glass of the cart barely obscure the piles of bouncy meatballs and delicately piled bunches of noodles waiting to be drowned in steaming, aromatic soup. This dish incorporates that feeling in a smaller package, using a wonton skin to mimic the noodle but still paying homage to the springy, funky meatball and its slippery, rich broth."

Pork Bakso Dumplings

ACTIVE 50 MIN; TOTAL 1 HR 25 MIN
SERVES 6

An aromatic blend of ground coriander, ginger, and lemongrass pairs with umami-rich fish sauce to season these delicate pork dumplings.

- 6   garlic cloves, chopped
- 1   (1½-inch) piece fresh ginger, peeled and chopped (about 2 Tbsp.)
- 2   Tbsp. thinly sliced lemongrass (from light end of 1 [2-oz.] stalk)
- 2½ Tbsp. fish sauce (such as Squid Brand)
- 1   tsp. granulated sugar
- ½   tsp. black pepper
- ½   tsp. ground coriander
- 1   lb. 80% lean ground pork
- 1   large egg white
- 2   Tbsp. ice water
- 40 dumpling wrappers
     Chile oil, for serving

1. Pulse garlic, ginger, and lemongrass in a food processor until finely chopped, about 5 pulses. Add fish sauce, sugar, pepper, and coriander, and pulse until combined, about 5 pulses. Add pork and egg white, and pulse until combined, about 6 pulses, stopping to scrape down sides of bowl as needed. With processor running, drizzle in 2 tablespoons ice water. Continue to process until mixture is emulsified and meat is lighter in color, 15 to 20 seconds.

2. Bring a large pot of water to a boil over high. Using wet hands, roll 1 tablespoon meat mixture into a ball. Place meatball on a baking sheet; repeat procedure with remaining meat mixture. Using your fingertip, lightly wet edges of 1 dumpling wrapper with water. Place 1 meatball slightly off-center in wrapper. Fold wrapper in half over meat, pressing edges tightly to seal and smoothing out any air pockets. Repeat with remaining wrappers and meatballs.

3. Place about one-fourth of dumplings in boiling water, and gently stir once. Boil until wrappers look glossy and dumplings float to surface and slightly puff up, about 8 minutes. Repeat 3 times with remaining dumplings.

4. To serve, place dumplings in a bowl, and drizzle with chile oil. —*TOM PISHA-DUFFLY, GADO GADO, PORTLAND, OREGON*

WINE Dry Australian Riesling: 2020 Jim Barry The Lodge Hill

NOTE Find fresh lemongrass stalks at South Asian markets.

▼

BUTTER UP
Chef English's original family recipe included more melted butter; drizzle with a little extra before baking, if desired.

EMBRACE FAMILY-STYLE COMFORT FOOD

KELLY ENGLISH   THE SECOND LINE, MEMPHIS

"I LOVE THIS DISH FOR TWO REASONS," says 2009 *Food & Wine* Best New Chef Kelly English. "First, the mirliton–or chayote, for those who don't speak Louisiana–is such a specific squash. You can't re-create it with anything else, and it just sings with seafood. Second, it is exactly where both of my parents' families come together in a casserole, at every table for almost every occasion."

Mirliton and Gulf Shrimp Casserole

ACTIVE 50 MIN; TOTAL 1 HR 50 MIN
SERVES 8

Mirliton, or chayote squash, tastes like a blend of cucumber and crisp zucchini. Paired with warming Creole seasoning and savory andouille sausage, the tender squash and sweet shrimp bring balancing freshness to this hearty casserole.

- 8   **cups water**
- 2   **Tbsp. plus ¼ tsp. kosher salt, divided**
- 2   **(10-oz.) mirlitons (chayote squash)**
- 1   **cup unsalted butter (8 oz.), plus more for drizzling (optional)**
- 8   **oz. smoked andouille sausage, halved lengthwise and cut into ½-inch-thick slices**
- 1   **medium-size yellow onion, chopped (about 1 cup)**
- 1   **medium-size green bell pepper, chopped (about 1 cup)**
- 2   **medium celery stalks, chopped (about 1 cup)**
- 2   **Tbsp. lower-sodium Creole seasoning**
- 4   **small garlic cloves, finely chopped**
- 2   **dried bay leaves**
- 1   **(12-oz.) fresh French bread loaf, torn into small pieces (about 12 cups)**
- 1   **lb. peeled and deveined raw small Gulf shrimp**
- 1   **bunch scallions, sliced (about 1 cup)**
- ½   **cup unsalted chicken stock**
- ½   **tsp. black pepper**
- 2   **oz. Parmesan cheese, shredded (about ½ cup)**

1. Bring 8 cups water and 2 tablespoons salt to a boil in a large saucepan over high. Reduce heat to low. Add mirlitons; cover and cook until tender, about 30 minutes. Fill a large bowl with ice water. Transfer mirlitons to ice water; let cool 5 minutes. Peel mirlitons; remove seeds. Chop mirlitons, and set aside.

2. Preheat oven to 350°F. Melt butter in a large Dutch oven over medium-high. Add andouille; cook until browned, 5 to 8 minutes. Using a slotted spoon, remove andouille; set aside. Reduce heat to low. Add mirlitons, onion, bell pepper, celery, Creole seasoning, garlic, and bay leaves. Cook, stirring occasionally, until mixture is very tender, about 25 minutes. Discard bay leaves. Stir in torn bread; cook, stirring constantly, until butter is absorbed, about 1 minute. Remove from heat; stir in andouille, shrimp, scallions, stock, pepper, and remaining ¼ teaspoon salt. Spoon into a 13- x 9-inch baking dish. Drizzle with additional melted butter, if desired; sprinkle with cheese. Bake in preheated oven until browned, about 20 minutes. —*KELLY ENGLISH, THE SECOND LINE, MEMPHIS*

WINE Brisk, lemony Sauvignon Blanc: 2020 Ancient Peaks Paso Robles

NOTE Find mirlitons at Latin American markets.

WINES FROM SPAIN

Journey in a Glass

For wine lovers, Spain offers the ultimate adventure, with grapes growing in nearly every nook of the country from the mountains to the sea. Here, over 200 native varieties, 139 designated wine regions, and 121,000+ hectares of organic vineyards crisscross the land, and locals appreciate life with a good bottle of vino. Sip your way through stellar regions, and discover a few stops you won't want to miss.

FWS ⟩ Foods and Wines from **Spain**

≈ alimentosdespaña

foodswinesfromspain.com/spainfoodnation

Delve into Green Spain & the Duero River Valley

Discover Albariño from the cool, misty climate of Green Spain in the northwest, facing the Atlantic Ocean—then expand your palate and explore prized red wines of the Duero River Valley to the east.

DO Rías Baixas

Mar de Frades Albariño Atlántico

With its iconic blue bottle symbolizing the modernity of Atlantic winemaking, this refreshing white wine honors the deeply rooted traditions of Albariño grapes. In the Galician language, its name means "Sea of Friars," a reference to the historic pilgrimage point where this sailboat-inspired winery now sits.

DO Toro

Vatán Tinta de Toro

Founded in 2010 by modern winemaking pioneer Jorge Ordóñez, the estate preserves ungrafted vineyards of Toro's oldest clones of Tinta de Toro. Vatán, the estate's flagship wine, exemplifies the fluid and elegant style of Toro, while maintaining the region's characteristic power and structure.

DO Ribera del Duero

Torres Celeste Crianza

With vines growing at 3,000 feet above sea level, this wine made from Tempranillo grapes has set its ambitions high, aiming to craft a bottle that's worthy of its terroir yet that keeps evolving, vintage after vintage. The results are big, with ripe black fruit and notes of coffee and dried plums.

Condado de Oriza Gran Reserva

Made from the very best Tempranillo grapes grown on 40-year-old vines, this wine is distinctive and special. Aged for 24 months in American and French oak barrels, and another 36 months in the bottle, it offers ripe berry fruits, balanced tannins, and a lovely long finish.

Tinto Pesquera Crianza

For more than 40 years, the Familia Fernández Rivera has been producing wines to please the most discerning palates. Exemplifying the ideal combination of elevation and well-drained soil, this wine is silky and sumptuous, with fresh aromatics and red berry fruit notes.

foodswinesfromspain.com/spainfoodnation

Explore the Ebro River Valley & Meseta

Best known for its red wine and Tempranillo grapes, where Rioja reigns supreme, the Ebro River Valley also produces many exciting whites and rosés. Another region worth adding to your radar is the expansive Meseta to the south, where organic vineyards abound.

DO La Mancha

Lobetia Single Vineyard Cabernet Sauvignon

Coming from the single estate of Dominio De Punctum, this biodynamic wine is produced without herbicides, pesticides, or animal products—making it vegan-friendly. After six months in American oak barrels, it's complex and fruity, with notes of blackberry and black cherry.

DOCa Rioja

Marqués de Cáceres Reserva

The carefully selected grapes, which are 85% Tempranillo and 15% Graciano and Garnacha, come from sun-soaked vineyards and old vines producing lower yields. To achieve a rich and velvety wine with great depth, it's barrel-aged for 22 months and two years in the bottle.

Muga Reserva

Merging family tradition and innovation, this winery hasn't lost any of its authenticity. With an on-site cooperage, it's the only winery in Spain that makes all of its vats and barrels. Here, old-world methods include racking casks by gravity and fining the wine with fresh egg whites.

Pata Negra Special Edition Crianza

This 12-month barrel-aged wine is refined enough to serve with a steak dinner or roast, but approachable enough to have with weeknight pizza. On the nose, red-fruit aromas combine with vanilla, clove, and aromatic herbs, and on the palate, this wine is tasty and structured.

Take Your Time in DO Cava

The history of Spanish fizz spans more than a century, and today Cava is at the forefront of quality sparkling wine. The first bottles of Cava were produced in 1872 using the *método tradicional* in the seaside town of Sant Sadurní d'Anoia, about an hour from Barcelona. Now, nearly 150 years later, this sparkling wine is governed by a strict set of guidelines and classifications that highlight the unique origins and long aging of Cavas.

Spanning from a "young" Cava de Guarda (aged in the bottle nine months) to the highest quality designation, Cava de Guarda Superior (aged for a minimum of 18 months and, by 2025, made with 100% organic grapes grown on vines at least 10 years old), Cavas are distinctive and versatile—the perfect pairing for any meal.

To learn more about Cava, visit **cava.wine/en**.

Cruise Down the Mediterranean Coast

From the once-obscure DOCa Priorat to the Capital of Cava, Spain's Mediterranean coast offers a wide range of styles and produces some of the world's most celebrated wines.

DO Cava

Anna de Codorníu Blanc de Blancs

Founded in 1551, Codorníu is Spain's oldest winery and considered by many to be the House of Cava. Its signature sparkling wine features a unique blend of Chardonnay and the three traditional Spanish varietals: Parellada, Xarel-lo, and Macabeu. The fine bubbles and creamy finish pair beautifully with food.

Parés Baltà Blanca Cusiné Gran Reserva Brut Nature

Hand-harvested, biodynamic Xarel-lo grapes—grown in the protected Parc del Foix mountains just south of Barcelona—play a starring role here, supported by Chardonnay and Pinot Noir. Aged for a minimum of 72 months in the bottle, it's a rare expression of finesse and elegance.

DOCa Priorat

Clos de Tafall Old Vines

Aged for 12 months in French oak barrels, this blend of old-vine Grenache, Carignan, and Cabernet Sauvignon is worthy of the Priorat appellation. Spice-tinged red and blue fruit and violet pastille flavors add complexity on the palate, leading to a long, precise finish with subtle tannins.

Get to know more about Spanish wines at **foodswinesfromspain.com/spainfoodnation**.

FOOD&WINE
SEEK & SAVOR
NEWS, UPDATES, EVENTS, AND MORE FROM **FOOD & WINE**

ATLANTIS BAHAMAS

Atlantis Paradise Island is the most remarkable resort destination in the world, with endless white-sand beaches, azure waters, and pools. Enjoy immersive marine experiences, Aquaventure water park, Ocean Club Golf Course, the Atlantis Casino, Mandara Spa, shopping, and entertainment.

AtlantisBahamas.com/FW
888.551.5519

TRY A REFRESHING PURE LEAF ICED TEA

At Pure Leaf, we say no to anything that doesn't make our iced tea better and yes to only the finest ingredients, expertly crafted. **No Artificial Sweeteners. No Artificial Flavors. No is Beautiful.**

Follow us @PureLeaf

VISIT FOOD & WINE

Foodandwine.com acts as your digital guide to the epicurean lifestyle. Visit us to discover inspiring and inclusive content on the culinary space, all things wine, the best of travel, and an elevated home environment.

FoodAndWine.com

Choucroute Pizzas

ACTIVE 15 MIN; TOTAL 2 HR
MAKES 2 (12-INCH) PIZZAS

Dijon mustard and tangy fermented sauerkraut cut through the creamy richness of melted fontina and mozzarella, while salty pistachios add a pleasant crunch to this Alsatian choucroute garnie–inspired pizza.

- 1 lb. fresh prepared pizza dough
- 3 Tbsp. Dijon mustard
- 2 Tbsp. heavy cream
  All-purpose flour, for work surface
- 3 oz. fresh mozzarella cheese, sliced
- 3 oz. young (aged 6 to 10 months) fontina cheese, thinly sliced
- 4 oz. thin mortadella deli slices
- ½ cup drained and squeezed dry jarred red or classic sauerkraut
- 2 Tbsp. chopped salted roasted pistachios

1. Let pizza dough stand at room temperature for 1 hour and 30 minutes. Meanwhile, position oven rack 6 inches from heat, and place a pizza stone on oven rack. Preheat oven to 500°F. Let pizza stone preheat in oven at least 30 minutes or up to 1 hour.

2. Stir together mustard and heavy cream in a small bowl. Divide dough in half on a lightly floured work surface. Roll and stretch half of dough into a 12-inch circle; place on a lightly floured sheet of parchment paper. Repeat process with remaining dough half. Spread mustard mixture evenly over dough circles, leaving a ¾-inch border. Top each dough circle with 1½ ounces mozzarella, 1½ ounces fontina, 2 ounces mortadella, and ¼ cup sauerkraut, leaving a ¾-inch border.

3. Increase oven temperature to high broil. Gently slide 1 pizza off parchment sheet and onto preheated pizza stone. Broil in preheated oven until well browned, 3 to 4 minutes. Using a pizza peel or rimless baking sheet, transfer cooked pizza to a platter or cutting board. Return pizza stone to oven, and let reheat 5 minutes. Repeat broiling process with second pizza. Sprinkle cooked pizzas evenly with pistachios. *—STEVEN DILLEY, BUFALINA, AUSTIN*

WINE Substantial, spicy Alsace white: 2017 Hugel & Fils Gewürztraminer

MAKE PIZZAS THAT CROSS BORDERS

STEVEN DILLEY   BUFALINA, AUSTIN

"**THE CHOUCROUTE PIE** was one of those ideas that felt obvious on arrival," says Steven Dilley, a 2017 *Food & Wine* Sommelier of the Year and owner of Bufalina in Austin. "The kitchen was sitting on some high-quality mortadella; it was fall, and my mind immediately went to Alsace. I love it because it has all those flavors that we love about the traditional dish–the rich mortadella and cheese offset by the assertive mustard and kraut–but it remains relatively balanced."

If you like farm-to-table,
you'll love ocean-to-plate.

Here in Key West, today's catch is often just that — caught today, grilled, broiled, blackened or sautéed before the next sunrise. And our dining venues? Just as enticing. From funky roadside fish stands to quaint bistros to elegant waterfront eateries. Then again, with the Atlantic on one side and Gulf of Mexico on the other, an infinite bounty of ocean-fresh delicacies is exactly what you'd expect.

fla-keys.com/keywest   1.800.527.8539

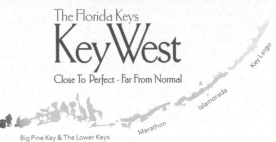

The Florida Keys
KeyWest
Close To Perfect - Far From Normal

Key Largo
Islamorada
Marathon
Big Pine Key & The Lower Keys

DO DINNER LIKE A BOSS

PAXX CARABALLO MOLL JUNGLE BAOBAO, SAN JUAN, PR

"I LOVE THE FLAVOR EXPLOSIONS and textures you get from this dish," says 2019 *Food & Wine* Best New Chef Paxx Caraballo Moll of Jungle BaoBao in San Juan, Puerto Rico. "Transforming a humble cut of meat, making it delicious, and seeing people's faces and all the great feedback make me proud of this dish. The sweetness of the carrots makes a great contrast with our gremolata, and every bite feels refreshing."

Skirt Steaks with Carrot Puree and Braised Cabbage

ACTIVE 45 MIN; TOTAL 55 MIN; SERVES 4

Velvety carrot puree, tender steak, and braised cabbage come together in a beautifully composed dish topped with a fresh, punchy cilantro gremolata. A well-prepared mise en place is the key here: Cut and measure ahead of time to cook and plate with ease.

- 1   cup chopped fresh cilantro
- ½   cup grapeseed oil
- 2   Tbsp. thinly sliced scallion
- 1¼ tsp. sambal oelek, divided
- 2   tsp. grated lemon zest plus ¼ cup fresh lemon juice, divided
- 1   Tbsp. plus ¼ tsp. kosher salt, divided
- 2   large carrots, roughly chopped (about 2 cups)
- 1   small russet potato, peeled and roughly chopped (about 1¼ cups)
- 8   cups thinly sliced red cabbage
- ½   cup packed light brown sugar
- ¼   tsp. ground cumin
- ½   cup soy sauce
- 2   (8-oz.) skirt steaks (¼ inch thick)
- 2   Tbsp. unsalted butter
- 2   tsp. honey
     Pickled Turmeric Onions (recipe follows)

1. Stir together cilantro, oil, scallion, 1 teaspoon sambal oelek, ½ teaspoon lemon zest, and ¼ teaspoon salt in a small bowl; set aside. Place carrots, potato, and remaining 1 tablespoon salt in a large saucepan; add water to cover by 1 inch. Bring to a boil over medium-high. Reduce heat to medium; cook until tender, about 15 minutes. Drain, reserving ½ cup cooking liquid. Place drained carrot mixture and ¼ cup reserved cooking liquid in blender. Secure lid; remove center piece to allow steam to escape. Place a kitchen towel over opening. Process until smooth, about 1 minute, adding additional cooking liquid, 1 tablespoon at a time, as needed to yield a silky-yet-firm texture. Set aside.

2. While carrots and potato boil, heat a large skillet over high. Add cabbage; cook, stirring often, until cabbage softens and darkens in color, about 4 minutes. Stir in brown sugar, cumin, and remaining ¼ teaspoon sambal oelek; cook, stirring constantly, until mixture starts to bubble, about 20 seconds. Reduce heat to medium-high. Stir in soy sauce; cook, stirring occasionally, until liquid is almost absorbed and cabbage is shiny, about 20 minutes. Reduce heat to low; cover to keep warm.

3. Heat a large cast-iron skillet over high. Add steaks; cook until a thermometer inserted into thickest portion registers 120°F, 5 to 6 minutes, flipping once halfway through cook time. Remove steaks from skillet; let rest 5 minutes. Cook carrot puree in a small saucepan over medium-high, stirring often, until heated through, 2 to 3 minutes. Reduce heat to medium-low. Add butter and honey; cook, stirring constantly, until emulsified, about 1 minute. Remove from heat.

4. Cut steaks against the grain into ¼-inch-thick slices; drizzle evenly with lemon juice, and sprinkle with remaining 1½ teaspoons lemon zest. Divide carrot puree evenly among 4 plates; top with sliced steak, cilantro gremolata, cabbage, and pickled turmeric onions. —*PAXX CARABALLO MOLL, JUNGLE BAOBAO, SAN JUAN, PUERTO RICO*

MAKE AHEAD Cabbage and carrot puree can be made up to 2 days ahead and stored in airtight containers in refrigerator.

WINE Ripe, low-tannin red: 2018 St. Francis Old Vines Zinfandel

Pickled Turmeric Onions

Combine 1½ cups sliced **white onion,** ¼ cup **fresh orange juice,** 2 tablespoons **rice vinegar,** ¼ teaspoon **kosher salt,** and ⅛ teaspoon **ground turmeric** in a bowl. Using hands, massage until onion softens and releases its juices, about 30 seconds. Cover and refrigerate up to 1 week.

INTRODUCING

MARTINI & ROSSI®
FIERO

— DAL 1863 —

A delicious low-ABV Aperitivo with
natural flavors of sweet hand-cut
Spanish orange peels.
Pair it with tonic
for a simple 50/50 Spritz.

BOTTLE SERVICE

COCKTAIL HOUR

The Soju Seer Master Sommelier Kyungmoon Kim found a new direction importing artisanal soju, the national spirit of Korea.

By Betsy Andrews

With rich, fermented sweetness and a golden amber color, Yangchon Chungju shines in the nutty, well-balanced Forever Young (recipe p. 95).

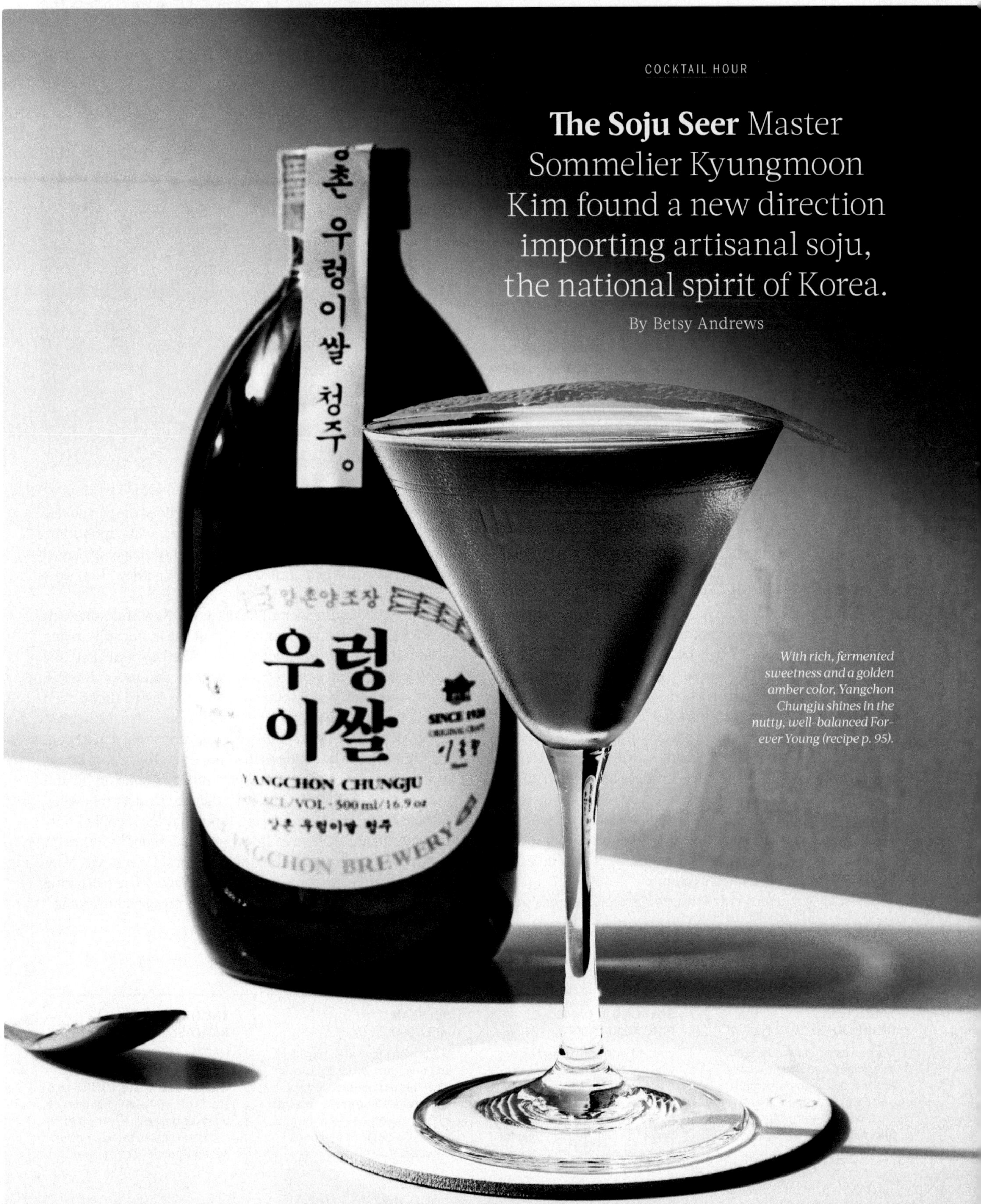

FOOD STYLING: RISHON HANNERS; PROP STYLING: CLAIRE SPOLLEN

produced by RAY ISLE *photography by* CAITLIN BENSEL

IN THE EARLY 2000S, Kyungmoon Kim found himself teaching wine-appreciation courses on South Korean warships. Kim had moved to the States from Korea as a teen and attended the Culinary Institute of America. There, students with prior restaurant experience outpaced him in the kitchen, but he excelled in the wine class. Encouraged, he went on to complete three levels of the Wine & Spirit Education Trust certification and pass the Court of Master Sommeliers' introductory and certified exams. And then he was required to serve in the South Korean navy.

"I was stuck on a base for two years, but I was determined to keep learning," he says. None of the wines in his coursework were available on the base, so he studied without tasting. He managed to win a sommelier competition in Seoul and started sharing his knowledge, offering seminars across the fleet. All the while, he was building the wine list for CIA classmate Jungsik Yim's first restaurant in Seoul, and after receiving his discharge, Kim started working there. When Yim opened Jungsik in New York City in 2011, Kim built that list, too.

Kim was enthusiastic about pairing wine with Korean cuisine. "We had close to a thousand labels," he says. But what he didn't anticipate was New Yorkers' interest in Korean drinks. In other Koreatown bars, the drink of choice was "green bottle" soju, a mass-produced spirit made with starches and additives. "I couldn't find anything I was proud to offer," he says. "But it stayed in the back of my mind."

In 2016, then working at The Modern, Kim passed the Court's Master Sommelier test, wine's most elite exam. "I thought, 'Now the world is going to open up for me,'" he remembers.

It didn't. He spent a year consulting for Dragonback Estate, a membership winery, in Argentina. He considered opening his own restaurant. "Then the light bulb came on," he says. Many of the restaurateurs he knew shared a need for an artisanal Korean beverage. So Kim hopped on a plane to Korea to discover what small rice distilleries were producing.

Koreans have been brewing cheongju–rice wine–for 2,000 years and distilling it into the spirit called soju since the 13th century. But in the 20th century, Japanese occupation and the Korean War left the country destitute, and what rice there was had to be used for food. Brewing and distilling rice were outlawed. Smaller operations shuttered; bigger ones turned to other grains, tapioca, or sweet potatoes for the base of their beverages. That went on for nearly half a century.

But when Kim returned to Korea, he learned that a renaissance

in soju was underway. The government had lifted the ban on rice distilling in the 1990s, eventually even bestowing upon some producers the title of Intangible Cultural Heritage. Artisanal soju was back. "When I tasted it, I was blown away," Kim says. "It opened my eyes."

Unlike the industrial stuff he'd seen in New York, the craft soju Kim tried was made in small batches in pot stills, using a natural yeast starter called nuruk. Whether bottled at 20% or 40% alcohol, they offered lush textures and notes of herbs, fruits, and cherry blossoms. But few had tasted them, even within Korea. The big, cheap bottles still dominated the market.

Kim decided to help small-scale producers find a market in the United States by acting as their importer. Today, Kim brings in soju that makes an elegant substitute for vodka or gin and pairs beautifully with food. Slowly, they're gaining a following.

"Soju is the most fascinating topic that few people know anything about," Kim says. He is optimistic about its future. "A lot of people hadn't yet learned about mezcal 15 years ago. Now, every restaurant has some from a little village. We're still taking baby steps with soju. But we can definitely get something going."

KYUNGMOON KIM'S PICKS
Find these at woorisoul.com.

YANGCHON CHUNGJU ($30)	**SOLSONGJU DAMSOUL PINE SOJU** ($26)	**SULSEAM MIR SOJU** ($30)	**THE HAN SEOUL NIGHT SOJU** ($17)
Brewed using glutinous rice, this golden rice wine is earthy and viscous, with mushroom, marzipan, and dried-pear flavors, plus a bittersweet nut-skin finish. Enjoy it alongside Korean barbecue.	Infused with spruce and pine, which is prized in Korea, and diluted with spruce tea, this herbaceous soju is a great swap for gin. Kim likes to stir it with Campari and Yangchon Chungju for a Korean spin on a Negroni.	Made with just water, nuruk, and rice from Gyeonggi province, this double-distilled spirit has a roasted-corn aroma and a lactic sweetness, with bright notes of pineapple and hops. It's wonderful on the rocks.	Made by distilling a liqueur created from golden plums and diluted to 23% alcohol, this soju starts off fruity but finishes with a tealike dryness. Try it with fish tacos or moules frites, or as an accompaniment to dessert.

White Gold

TOTAL 5 MIN; SERVES 1

This sweet-and-sour cocktail calls to mind the tart creaminess of a gin fizz but brings the punchier, grain-forward notes of Golden Barley 40 soju in place of floral gin. The frothy egg white cuts through those brightly boozy and acidic flavors to balance each sip.

¼ cup (2 oz.) Golden Barley 40 soju

1½ Tbsp. fresh lemon juice (about ¾ oz.)

1½ Tbsp. (¾ oz.) Cointreau

1 large egg white

Lemon peel twist

Edible gold leaf (optional)

Combine Golden Barley soju, lemon juice, Cointreau, and egg white in a cocktail shaker; place lid on shaker, and shake until egg white is frothy, about 20 seconds. Add ice to fill shaker; place lid on shaker, and shake until drink is chilled, about 15 seconds. Strain into a coupe glass. Garnish with lemon peel twist and, if desired, edible gold leaf. —*KYUNGMOON KIM*

NOTE Golden Barley 40 soju can be purchased at woorisoul.com.

Forever Young

PHOTO P. 93

TOTAL 5 MIN; SERVES 1

Inspired by the classic Adonis cocktail of sherry and vermouth, this stiff drink balances earthy, fermented Yangchon Chungju with amaro. Both offer a pleasantly musky, nutty flavor, and vermouth shines through with a burst of sweetness.

3 Tbsp. (1½ oz.) Yangchon Chungju

2 Tbsp. (1 oz.) Cocchi Vermouth di Torino (sweet vermouth)

1 Tbsp. (½ oz.) Amaro Nonino Quintessentia

2 dashes orange bitters

1 (3- x 1-inch) orange peel strip

Combine Yanchgon Chungju, Cocchi Vermouth di Torino, Amaro Nonino Quintessentia, and orange bitters in an ice-filled mixing glass; stir until drink is chilled, 30 to 45 seconds. Strain into a Nick and Nora glass. Garnish with orange peel strip. —*KYUNGMOON KIM*

NOTE Yangchon Chungju can be purchased at woorisoul.com.

WHAT TO DRINK NOW

The Perfect Pizza Pairings, Please? Push your pizza boundaries and match wines to toppings.

By Ray Isle

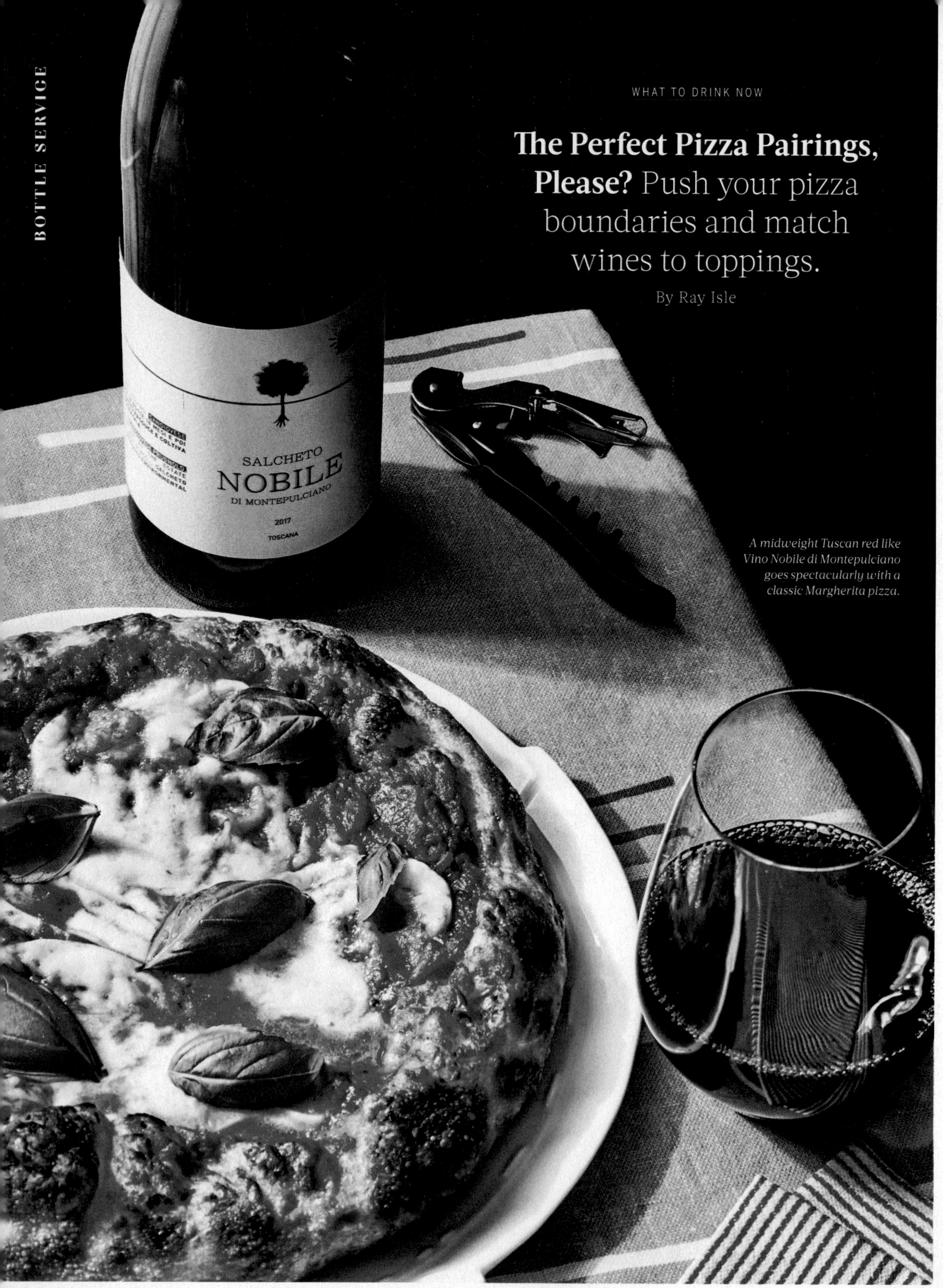

A midweight Tuscan red like Vino Nobile di Montepulciano goes spectacularly with a classic Margherita pizza.

FOOD STYLING: RISHON HANNERS; PROP STYLING: CLAIRE SPOLLEN

photography by CAITLIN BENSEL

BELLE GLOS

THE BEAUTY OF PINOT

THE WHITE PIZZA
+ Sparkling Rosé

PIZZA IS THE ULTIMATE CASUAL, fun food, which probably explains why people in the U.S. eat something around 3 billion pizzas every year. (That's right: *3 billion.*) Given its ubiquity, dwelling too much on which wine pairs best with which pizza could seem a bit like perhaps you're missing the point. You want Sauvignon Blanc with your spicy soppressata pie? An IPA? A shot of tequila? Chocolate milk? Hey, go for it.

But thinking about wine pairings is, believe it or not, fun (at least if you don't take it too seriously), and the truth is that a wine that goes amazingly well with a veggie pizza topped with green peppers and broccoli might not be the one that sings out in harmony with a meat lover's pepperoni-sausage-ham extravaganza (far more fat in the latter: good with red wine tannins). As Randall Restiano, the beverage director at Serra by Birreria in New York City's Eataly, says, "Pizza and wine are among my favorite things to pair, but obviously, the toppings make a world of difference."

He's right (and I know that partly because he sent over about 10 different pies to our tasting to prove the point). So, for anyone who's game, here are a few proposals that will push your pizza-wine experience into perfection.

THE WHITE PIE DIVIDES PEOPLE: Some love it, and some just walk away wondering what the heck happened to the tomato sauce. Regardless, losing the acidity that tomatoes provide changes the pairing equation. The gentle fruitiness and tingly bubbles of sparkling rosé work perfectly here.

NV LE MONDE SPARKLING PINOT NERO *($20)*

Sparkling rosé Pinot Noir from Italy's Friuli region? Well, why not—especially when it's as appealing as this vibrant wine is.

NV VALDO MARCA ORO PROSECCO ROSÉ *($15)*

This dry, zesty sparkling rosé from Italy's Prosecco region recalls the rosés of Provence: watermelon, strawberry, and a little raspberry.

NV SEGURA VIUDAS CAVA BRUT ROSÉ *($15)*

Spanish Cava is superb with a slice of Manchego and bread, and what is a white pizza but bread covered in melted cheese? Segura Viudas' rosé version is delightful.

NV BILLECART-SALMON CHAMPAGNE BRUT ROSÉ *($89)*

Who says Champagne has to be reserved for fancy foods like caviar? Billecart's elegant rosé is pricey, but why not try a half-bottle for date night?

ONE GOOD
SIN LEADS
TO ANOTHER

NEW

7 Deadly® Cab

PERFECT WITH PEPPERONI
+ Bold, Spicy Reds

THERE'S SUCH JOY to be found in those upturned cups of heat-blasted pepperoni on the most popular pizza style in the U.S. There's also the (admittedly delicious) glistening oil that cured meats like pepperoni and soppressata release as they cook. Look for reds with some tannic oomph to balance the fat.

2017 DOW VALE DO BOMFIM DOURO *($12)*

Made from varieties like Touriga Nacional typically used for port wine, this purple-hued Portuguese red is full of ripe berry fruit and soft, mouth-coating tannins. A hint of violets lifts the aroma.

2018 CANTINA COLOSI NERO D'AVOLA SICILIA *($15)*

Terraced vineyards near the southern coast of Sicily provide the grapes for this dark-fruited, structured red—think black cherries and plums, fermented and aged entirely in stainless steel.

2019 CARLISLE SONOMA COUNTY ZINFANDEL *($31)*

For this powerful, spicy red, winemaker Mike Officer uses fruit from the vineyards—some over 100 years old—that go into his acclaimed single-vineyard bottlings. (And if you love this wine, get on the Carlisle mailing list for his more limited ones.)

2017 PASQUA PASSIONESENTIMENTO ROSSO *($16)*

This abundantly flavorful Veronese red uses the primary grape of Amarone, Corvina, at its core. It's full-bodied and rich—if there were such a thing as a wild boar ragù pizza, this would be your go-to.

SAVOUR
THE WORLD
WITHOUT LEAVING THE RESORT

★★★★★
5-STAR
GLOBAL GOURMET™
SAVOUR THE WORLD

THE GOLD STANDARD ALL INCLUSIVE DINING™

MASTERS OF EXCELLENCE IN THE CULINARY ARTS

UP TO **16** RESTAURANTS PER RESORT

SANDALS® HAS MORE RESTAURANTS PER GUEST THAN ANY OTHER CARIBBEAN RESORTS

At Sandals Resorts, each and every dish is passionately created by internationally trained chefs using only fresh, top-quality ingredients, boat-to-table seafood, and superior meats grilled to perfection, all while you enjoy a setting as authentic as the cuisine. You will discover a gastronomic journey featuring up to 23 unique culinary concepts from around the world, and premium brand liquors, without ever leaving the resort. And our always smiling, endlessly hospitable staff is on hand to provide a level of service that is simply incomparable, anywhere. It's all part of the 5-Star Luxury Included® experience, and just one more way Sandals demonstrates its commitment to offering our guests only the best of everything.

Sandals®
f ⊙ 𝕏 P ▶ @sandalsresorts

SANDALS.COM • 1.800.SANDALS
OR CALL YOUR TRAVEL ADVISOR

THE WORLD'S BEST SERVES THE WORLD'S BEST

VOTED WORLD'S BEST **25** YEARS IN A ROW AT THE WORLD TRAVEL AWARDS

JAMAICA I ANTIGUA I SAINT LUCIA I THE BAHAMAS I GRENADA I BARBADOS I CURAÇAO (2022)

Sandals® is a registered trademark. Unique Vacations, Inc. is an affiliate of Unique Travel Corp., the worldwide representative of Sandals Resorts.

CLASSIC CHEESE
+ Pinot, Chianti, and Friends

WHETHER IT'S A PLAIN CHEESE from Domino's or a Margherita made with buffalo mozzarella, extra-virgin olive oil, and tomatoes straight from the slopes of Mount Vesuvius, the key here is simplicity (and not that much fat). Chianti Classico really does work like a charm, but so do other midweight reds, like Vino Nobile di Montepulciano or even Pinot Noir from Oregon.

2018 BADIA A COLTIBUONO CHIANTI CLASSICO *($22)*

Chianti Classico refers to the region itself, not the style, but there's no question that this is spot-on Chianti Classico: crisp acidity, notes of dried herbs, wild berry flavors. It's a great weeknight dinner wine.

2017 SALCHETO VINO NOBILE DI MONTEPULCIANO *($24)*

A short distance across the Tuscan countryside from Chianti lies the Vino Nobile di Montepulciano appellation. Sangiovese here tends to be riper and richer, and this wine from Salcheto—made from organically farmed grapes—is characteristic, with robust dark fruit.

2018 ROSEROCK EOLA–AMITY HILLS PINOT NOIR *($32)*

Pinot with pizza? Why not! The fine tannins and savory notes that Pinot grapes attain in Oregon's Willamette Valley make it an ideal partner. This spicy, medium-bodied wine from Domaine Drouhin's Roserock estate is a go-to choice.

2019 BERNABELEVA CAMINO DE NAVAHERREROS *($18)*

Grenache from Spain's Gredos region, near Madrid, tends toward supple elegance, with bright, red-fruit flavors and firm minerality. This one hits the target.

THE VEGGIE PIE
+ Crisp, Chillable Reds

WHEN WE TASTE-TESTED a range of pizzas with a slew of wines from around the world at the F&W offices, we found that the No. 1 fave for a veggie-topped pizza was a light-bodied and (if you want) chillable red. The crisp zip of the wine was inarguably excellent with zucchini, broccoli, arugula, and more. Light Italian reds like Piedmont's Freisa grape were standouts, but there are plenty of other options.

2019 J. LOHR WILDFLOWER VALDIGUIÉ *($10)*

Almost no one grows Valdiguié (once known as "Napa Gamay") in California anymore, but J. Lohr has been at it with determination for decades. Moderate in alcohol and full of lively pomegranate and pepper flavors, it's a total pleasure.

2018 PIO CESARE BARBERA D'ALBA *($27)*

Pio Boffa, the irrepressible force behind this historic Piedmontese producer's wines, passed away this year from COVID, a terrible loss. But his family will keep the winery going (as it has for five generations now), making wines like this cherry-spicy Barbera. Raise a toast to him with it.

2018 FRATELLI ALESSANDRIA VERDUNO PELAVERGA SPEZIALE *($28)*

This plummy Pelaverga comes from a family who has been making wine in the area since 1870; they're masters of this unusual grape.

2018 VIETTI FREISA VIVACE *($28)*

Lightly tingly, bursting with ripe raspberry notes, and just generally full of life, this Piedmontese red from acclaimed Barolo winemaker Luca Currado is a delight to drink— serve it lightly chilled.

FOOD STYLING: EMILY NABORS HALL

SHOPPING A LA CARTE

No Peeling, No Chopping, No Mess. **Dorot Gardens** are pre-portioned frozen garlic, onions and herbs cubes to effortlessly flavor up your marinades, dips and more. Add healthy flavor fast to meals & snacks without the mess.

Dorotgardens.com

DID YOU KNOW TAHINI IS A SUPER-FOOD? Protein packed, creamy, **Mighty Sesame Organic Tahini** is just 1 crazy delicious ingredient readily versatile to zest up smoothies, dips, baking & more, in a convenient squeeze bottle. Try all three flavors Organic, Whole Seed, and Harissa. Available on Amazon.com and

mightysesame.com

Green Tea: It's all in the Leaves!

Available for purchase with coupon in fine stores everywhere or online at:

www.appliednutrition.com
Enter Coupon Code: 014703

SUPER CENTERS · SAFEWAY · WHOLESALE CLUB · CVS/pharmacy · meijer · RITE AID

GREEN TEA FAT BURNER
SAVE $1
EXPIRES 12/31/21   MANUFACTURERS COUPON

Consumer: Redeemable at retail locations only. Not valid for online or mail-order purchases. Retailer: Irwin Naturals will reimburse you for the face value plus 8 (cents) handling provided it is redeemed by a consumer at the time of purchase on the brand specified. Coupons not properly redeemed will be void and held. Reproduction by any party by any means is expressly prohibited. Any other use constitutes fraud. Irwin Naturals reserves the right to deny reimbursement (due to misredemption activity) and/or request proof of purchase for coupon(s) submitted. Mail to: CMS Dept. 10363, Irwin Naturals, 1 Fawcett Drive, Del Rio, TX 78840. Cash value: .001 (cents). Void where taxed or restricted. ONE COUPON PER PURCHASE. Not valid for mail order/websites. Retail only.

0710363-014703

These statements have not been evaluated by the Food & Drug Administration. This product is not intended to diagnose, treat, cure or prevent any disease.

FortunaSausage.com
800-42SOUPY 800-427-6879

SHIPPING NATIONWIDE DAILY

FREE U.S. SHIPPING

The BlendJet portable blender delivers game-changing technology that lets you make fresh smoothies and protein shakes wherever you go. It crushes ice & frozen fruit, is quiet, water-resistant & self-cleaning! Comes in 20 colors. Free 2-Day S&H.

Save 11% at blendjet.com/foodwine

HAND CRAFTED ALL-NATURAL
CHILI SAUCE
FROM OUR FAMILY TO YOURS!

A unique blend of savory, sweet, and just the right amount of spice, **Me's Way Chili sauce** is the first choice for every chili sauce connoisseur who tries it!

Available in Regular and Vegan, 8 oz. and 16 oz. **FREE Shipping** for all orders within the U.S. **Take $5 off** for an additional 8 oz. **or $10 off** for an additional 16 oz.

meswayllc.com

To advertise: contact Devin at MI Integrated Media, 860-542-5180 or devin@mi-ms.com

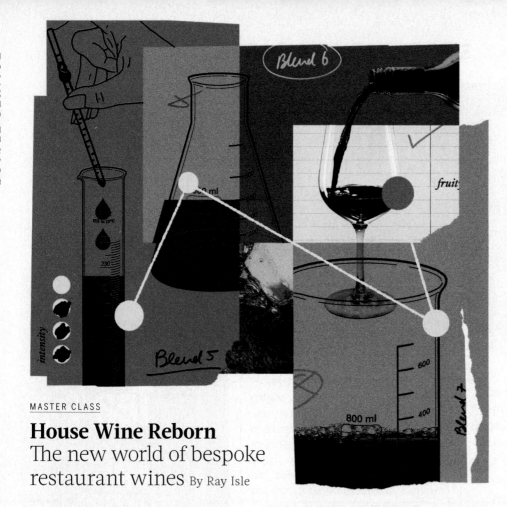

MASTER CLASS

House Wine Reborn
The new world of bespoke restaurant wines By Ray Isle

WAY BACK WHEN, I used to go to an elderly French bistro for dinner sometimes with an equally elderly friend of my mother-in-law. The place was called Le Veau d'Or (acquired recently by the team behind NYC's Frenchette, with plans for revivification). It was the old school's idea of old-school: one gloomy, stooped waiter in a jacket, tripes à la mode de Caen and veal kidneys on the menu, and a house red served from a big screw-cap bottle kept below the bar. That wine was not good. I kept to steak au poivre and ordered bourbon. So did Mrs. L., my mother-in-law's friend. She also smoked cigarettes at the table. No one told her not to. She was 85 and mean.

Things change. Mrs. L. left this earth for heaven–I'm sure God doesn't tell her what she can or can't do either–and recently, I sat in on a blending session for a house wine that Hirsch Vineyards makes for Tennessee's Blackberry Mountain. Winemaker Jasmine Hirsch and Blackberry Mountain's Andy Chabot and Logan Griffin went through samples from 10 different barrels (out of 280) from Hirsch's 2020 vintage, saying things like (Chabot) "The '18 Stockinger from 8A1 smells a little dark, then it's zippy and zesty and really kinda cool," and (Hirsch) "Can I make a suggestion? I think with this blend you've kind of nailed it on the fruit. But I might try it without the 6C." No screw-cap jugs here.

In other words, the new world of house wines is very different from the old. Call them bespoke restaurant wines. To make them, wine directors work directly with wineries to create cuvées that work particularly well with the restaurant's menu. For instance, Chabot's goal was to create a wine that would be consumed soon after release rather than cellared. So, tasting today, he's asking himself, "What do we think is going to be pleasing a year from now for a guest? We have to think of it as a primary thing. It has to appeal to people right off the bat." For Paul Einbund at The Morris in San Francisco, the idea was an immediately drinkable California red he could pour by the ounce (fun idea); the result, a lively, blueberry-accented blend of robust red varieties from the Sierra Foothills. These are only two of many.

And at the blending trial for Blackberry Mountain, work goes on. After tasting through each of the 10 samples separately–from different barrels and different blocks of the vineyard–Hirsch, Chabot, and Griffin now go through eight trial blends, assembling them with graduated cylinders, pouring carefully, and then tipping them into glasses. It's all nuance (and all very good). Almost done. Until Chabot says, "I think blend number six is pretty darn good. Really good. But I'd hate to just stop there–if we tried adding a little of the 11C, just to lift the freshness … "

DRINK THE HOUSE

Nine top bespoke restaurant wines to order the next time you dine

Union Square Hospitality Group, NYC
2013 Il Baccante Toscana Rosso
(made by Vecchie Terre di Montefili)

The Nicolett, Lubbock, Texas
NV House Red
(made by Kim McPherson of McPherson Cellars)

The Kahala Hotel & Resort, Honolulu
Donson Champagne
(made by La Maison Donson)

Fogo de Chão, various locations
2018 Eulila Cachapoal Valley Red
(made by Viña Vik)

The Morris, San Francisco
NV House Red
(made by Miraflores Winery)

Blackberry Mountain, Walland, Tennessee
2019 Hirsch Vineyards, Estate, Pinot Noir, Blackberry Mountain Edition
(made by Hirsch Vineyards)

RPM Steak, Chicago
2016 Les Chèvres Napa Valley Cabernet Sauvignon
(made by Checkerboard Vineyard)

City Winery, various locations
2018 Pinot Noir Reserve, Cuvée Bacigalupi
(made by City Winery, fruit from Bacigalupi Vineyards in Sonoma County)

Cote, NYC
2019 Piora Syrah
(made by Presqu'ile Winery, fruit from Camp 4 Vineyard)

illustration by RICARDO SANTOS

CLASSIC WINES

With three days of cooking demonstrations and wine tastings led by some of the industry's top chefs and wine experts, the 2021 FOOD & WINE Classic in Aspen was the culinary event of the year. Bring some of that excitement home with this exclusive wine guide, which introduces some of the superb bottles sampled under the tents.

J VINEYARDS & WINERY

Sonoma Style

Set in the heart of Sonoma County, J Vineyards & Winery invites you to experience the beauty, flavor, and style of California's iconic Russian River Valley.

—

Surrounded by terraced vineyards and sun-drenched hillsides, J Vineyards & Winery offers an exceptional California wine country experience—whether you're indulging in the five-course tasting menu in the winery's exclusive Bubble Room or hosting a celebratory wine tasting at home.

THE VINEYARDS

Founded more than 35 years ago on land selected for its unique soil and ideal climate, this innovative winery blends traditional and modern methods. The J winemaking team, led by Nicole Hitchcock, are true stewards of the land. Explains Hitchcock: "Crafting wine requires relentless dedication, a passion for problem-solving, fearlessness of getting dirty, and true team spirit."

THE EXPERIENCE

If you find yourself in Sonoma County, a visit to J Vineyards & Winery is a must. The warm hospitality, innovative culinary pairing experiences, and chic tasting spaces provide the perfect way to sample the winemaking team's celebrated portfolio. Hitchcock recommends the Legacy Tasting, which includes the option of five cheeses, each topped with their own house-made accompaniments—"anything from spiced fresh fruits with roasted almonds, to sesame-brown butter nut brittle, to a silky chocolate fudge," she says. "It pairs beautifully with both our varietal and sparkling flights, highlighting different flavors and textures with each wine."

TASTING NOTES

For a decadent tasting at home, try these pairing suggestions with wines that were featured in the Grand Tasting Pavilion at the 2021 FOOD & WINE Classic in Aspen this September.

J CUVÉE 20 BRUT NV: An elegant and lively sparkling wine offering a complex palate, balancing notes of baked apple and nectarine with hints of toasted chestnut. Enjoy a glass with seared black cod and caramelized cauliflower.

2018 RUSSIAN RIVER VALLEY PINOT NOIR: Approachable, balanced, and velvety smooth—look for notes of berry and pomegranate that give way to hints of anise and cola. Pair it with grilled pork chops in a peach-bourbon glaze.

Uncork the entire line of J sparkling and still varietals at **JWine.com**.

WINES OF ITALY

Fabulous Finds from Italy

Home to some of the oldest wine-producing regions in the world, Italy offers a wonderfully diverse range of wines—with varieties and styles for every palate, occasion, and budget.

—

Did you know that Italy produces wine in every one of its 20 geographical regions? Or that it is home to more indigenous grape varieties than any other country on the planet? The world of Italian wine is not just varied, it's endlessly vast! For wine lovers, this means exploring Italian wine is not just a mere pastime, it's a journey—an exciting adventure where there is always a new varietal to taste, another region to discover, a different style to observe. Get started on your dive into Italian wine with these five remarkable wines, most of which are featured at the 2021 FOOD & WINE Classic in Aspen.

One of the most famous Crus in Gavi is **Villa Sparina's Monterotondo.**

Villa Sparina

In the heart of Piedmont, about an hour from the cool breezes of the Mediterranean Sea, lies the picture-perfect Villa Sparina estate. Boasting some of the region's most favorable terroir for producing the Cortese grape, the estate is, of course, renowned for its distinct Gavi wines, including the award-winning **Monterotondo cru.** An age-worthy Riserva, this wine leads with a stone and mineral thread, followed by ripe lemon and peaches. Its rich texture and crisp acidity pair well with steamed shellfish, grilled seafood, or sushi. *villasparinaresort.it/en*

Fattoria le Pupille is led by a mother-and-daughter team; mother Elisabetta Geppetti, the "Lady of Morellino," is the Ambassador of Maremma.

Fattoria le Pupille

Situated in Maremma, in southern Tuscany, Fattoria le Pupille is a pioneer in the world of Super Tuscan wines. Elisabetta Geppetti, who oversees the winery with her daughter, Clara Gentili, credits her father-in-law "Fredi" as her mentor and great inspiration. His namesake label **Saffredi** has become an iconic Super Tuscan and recently celebrated three decades of top scores and reviews. The 2015 vintage boasts an intense color and deep concentration of red fruits. Look for spicy, balsamic notes on the palate, dense tannins, and a rich mouth feel. It pairs beautifully with red meat and game, as well as dark chocolate. *fattorialepupille.it/en*

I Greppi

Founded by two of Tuscany's most famous winemaking families, the I Greppi estate comprises three separate parcels, each with a distinct soil type, in the heart of the Bolgheri DOC, the spiritual homeland of the Super Tuscan movement. The winery's proximity to the coast makes it ideal for allowing extended ripening, which ultimately leads to bold, full-bodied wines. **Greppicaia** is a spectacular Super Tuscan, crafted from the estate's best grapes. Rich and decadent, it brims with dark berries, incense, and black tea. It's the perfect accompaniment to a hearty main course such as lamb osso buco, roast beef, or lasagna. *igreppi.com*

I Greppi is located in Bolgheri, one of the most prestigious wine areas of Italy, where some of the best Tuscan wines are produced.

Cà dei Frati

In the southern part of Lake Garda, in a valley surrounded by mineral-rich hills, Cà dei Frati has been producing haute-qualité wines since 1939. Owned and operated by the Dal Cero family, the winery is a leading producer of Lugana, an elegant and structured white wine crafted from 100% native Turbiana grapes. For an exemplary introduction to this unique varietal, try **Cà dei Frati Brolettino**, an aged Lugana that features aromas of melon and apple, followed by hints of cedar and toast. On the palate, you can expect ripe peach and grapefruit, which means it will pair beautifully with poultry, shellfish, or a creamy pasta. *cadeifrati.it/en*

Cà dei Frati Brolettino Lugana is aged for 10 months in barriques and three months in the bottle.

Movia

Uniquely situated in the Slovenian village of Ceglo, just a stone's throw from the Italian border, Movia is a family-owned winery that dates to 1820. Renowned for its dedication to organic and biodynamic farming, the estate cultivates grapes without herbicides, pesticides, or fungicides, and crafts wines naturally, without unnecessary interference from the winemaker. **Movia Lunar** is a rich, full-bodied white made from Chardonnay and Ribolla grapes. Deeply golden in color, due to eight months of maceration (when the grape skins stay in contact with the juice), it has a long and flavorful finish with subtle notes of apricot and ground clove. Enjoy it with a robust dish such as roast veal or braised lamb shanks. *movia.si/en*

Movia is one of the first modern wineries to follow biodynamic principles since the 19th century.

WINE.COM

The Classic Delivered to Your Door

This fall, high-profile chefs, renowned winemakers, and food lovers alike convened for one of the most eagerly awaited festivals of the year: The Food & Wine Classic in Aspen. For three days, they cooked, they tasted, and they learned together through live demos, wine tastings, and discussions.

For home cooks and wine lovers, the spirit of the Classic continues well beyond Aspen and into everyday kitchens and dining rooms through mouthwatering meals and wine pairings. Thanks to Wine.com, you too can bring the wines and flavors of the Grand Tasting Pavilion home when you order from their vast selection. Taste wines from the festival, recreate the seminars, or explore and learn on your own with help from the world's largest wine store.

Seminar Spotlight:
FROM CAVA TO SEKT: WORLD-CLASS SPARKLING WINES
Go beyond Champagne and discover a world of bubbly when you explore the lesser known but no-less noteworthy sparkling wines from renowned regions. Uncork a bottle of Spanish Cava, German Sekt, Italian Prosecco, and French Crémant to taste the array of styles and production methods that comprise world-class sparkling wine. See if you can note the subtle differences among the wines, such as bubble size, aromas, and flavors, to develop your palate for the sparkly stuff. Invite friends to taste along with you to learn together and create a Classic moment at home. Shop Sparkling Wine at **wine.com/sparkling**.

THE SPIRIT OF THE CLASSIC ON YOUR OWN
Explore and build your palate at Wine.com. With the largest selection of critically acclaimed and boutique wines from around the globe, there are new discoveries waiting for every wine lover. Get started by perusing the list of wines poured in Aspen or chat with a wine expert for personalized recommendations. Shop the Classic at **wine.com/theclassic**.

Make a Classic Charcuterie Board

Served as an appetizer or even a snacky meal, a charcuterie board allows you to explore the ways flavors mingle and complement each other.

Food-Friendly Reds

Low to medium body red wines offer balanced tannins and high acidity, which makes them easy to pair with a wide array of cheeses, cured meats, nuts, and dried fruit. A classic selection of gouda, Gruyère, salami, and mortadella would pair well with Pinot Noir, Montepulciano, and Grenache.

Palate-Refreshing Sparklers

Bubbles and bites work well together because effervescent wines help brighten heavier cheeses, such as a creamy brie and Champagne, or charcuterie with ribbony fat, such as prosciutto and Prosecco. For a colorful spread, try sparkling Rosé with a sharp cheddar, aged Manchego, or Jamón Ibérico, a rich Spanish ham.

Crowd-Pleasing Whites

Versatile, full-bodied white wines, like Chardonnay or Viognier, have the complexity to stand up to the pungent flavors like blue cheese and truffle-infused salami. Fruity and acidic whites, such as Sauvignon Blanc and Riesling, also play nicely with spice and smoke like a spicy chorizo.

Bring the Classic Home with Wine.com.

Get free shipping and endless wine discovery all year when you join StewardShip for $49. **Learn more at wine.com/ StewardShip.**

wine.com

PHOTO BY MATT WILSON

WINES OF CHILE

Spectacular & Sustainable

Nestled in valleys between the soaring Andes mountains and the Pacific coastline, Chile's diverse wine regions produce some of the world's most remarkable—and sustainable—wines.

While Chile's many wine regions vary both in geography and climate, Chilean wine farmers are united in their commitment to protecting the environment and preserving the land's precious natural resources. Start exploring Chile's exceptional array of sustainably produced wines with these three vintages, which were spotlighted at the 2021 FOOD & WINE Classic in Aspen.

DON MELCHOR 2018

An icon of Chilean wine, this world-class Cabernet Sauvignon has been paving the way for Chile's fine wines for more than 30 years. The 2018 vintage exhibits great personality and complexity, balancing small red fruits with floral notes. On the palate, expect well-integrated tannins and a long, refined finish. Pair it with lamb, wild game, pâtés, and mature cheeses. *DonMelchorUS.com*

TRIPLE C 2017

A Chilean interpretation of a Bordeaux Blend (Cabernet Franc, Cabernet Sauvignon and Carménère), Triple C is one of five ultra-premium wines produced by acclaimed winery, Viña Santa Rita. The 2017 Triple C highlights the elegance of Cabernet Franc. Deep ruby-red in color, it boasts intense aromas of black cherry and dark chocolate, with cedar and tobacco notes. Enjoy it with a hearty pasta dish, roasted poultry, or veal stew. *SantaRita.com*

MONTES PURPLE ANGEL 2018

A pioneer in the Colchagua Valley—one of Chile's most acclaimed wine regions—Viña Montes is one of the country's most recognizable wine estates. Montes Purple Angel represents a whole new dimension for Carménère, a Bordeaux grape varietal. The 2018 vintage features aromas of ripe red and black berries, dark chocolate, and coffee. Well-structured, with smooth and full tannins, it pairs harmoniously with red meats and cheeses. *MontesWines.com*

FOOD & WINE
classic in aspen
SEPTEMBER 10-12, 2021

F&W is thrilled to welcome these amazing partners to the Grand Tasting Pavilion at the FOOD & WINE Classic in Aspen. Take a tour of the tents with this list as your guide and sample some of the best wines, spirits and foods from around the globe. Enjoy your food and wine!

······· EXHIBITORS ·······

00 Wines
Alpha Omega Collective
ARANO
Archer Roose
Argaux
AS ONE CRU
Athletic Brewing Company
Bardstown Bourbon Company
Basil Hayden
Bee Hunter
Belle Glos
Benovia Winery
Biagio Cru Wines
Blackland Distillery
Böen
BORGOGNO
Bovine & Swine Meats
Brandlin Estate & Cuvaison
Bravo
California Wineries & Vineyards - Tobias Glen Vineyard
Cape Classics
Carboy Winery
CarryOn
Casa de Valor
Casa Del Sol Tequila
Château Minuty
Citation - Centerstone Wines

Código 1530 Tequila
Coravin
Crown Point Vineyards
Davos Brands
DiNoci Dairy Free Ice Cream
Discover Puerto Rico
Doña Vega Mezcal
Duhig Wine
Elouan
Epicurean Butter
Ethica Wines
Far Niente Family of Wineries
Field Recordings.
Five Trail Blended American Whiskey
Fords Gin
Frankly Organic Vodka
Frescobaldi Toscana
Gloria Ferrer Winery
Grain & Barrel Spirits
Gratien & Meyer Cremant
Greenbar Distilling
Grounded Wine Co.
Grüvi
Halyard Brewing Company
Hawk and Horse Vineyards
Hedley & Bennett
Imagery Wine Collection
Irvine & Roberts Vineyards

J Vineyards and Winery
Jägermeister Cold Brew Coffee
K Vintners / HOUSE OF SMITH
Kendall-Jackson
Kerrygold
Kosta Browne Winery
KREWE
La Adelita Tequila
La Scolca & Sartori di Verona
La Vita Bella
LALO
LangeTwins Family Winery
Lions Head Collection
Liquore Strega
Lobos 1707
Lord Jones
M Imports
Madre Mezcal
Maestro Dobel
Maison Ferrand
Marriot Bonvoy® American Express®
Martha Stewart Kitchen Foods
Maytag Dairy Farms
Mendocino Wine Company
Michael David Winery
Mr Black Spirits
Mt. Beautiful
Napa Valley Quilt

NORTH BERKELEY IMPORTS
Nowadays
Nubocha Dairy Free Gelato
Old Bridge Cellars
Oshēn Salmon
Pacaso
PAMA Liqueur
Pint's Peak Ice Cream
PKGD Group
POM Wonderful
Pyramid Valley
Quigley Fine Wines
Red Belly Honey
Roadhouse Brewing Company
Rombauer Vineyards
Roots Run Deep Winery
Sans Wine Co.
Santa Margherita USA
Santa Teresa Rum
Scheid Family Wines
SHARE A SPLASH wine co.
Silverado Vineyards
Sinegal Estate
Snowmass Mountain Club
Spire Collection
St. Vrain Cidery
Stag's Leap Wine Cellars
Stranahan's
Stratus Wine & Spirits

Teremana Tequila
The Calling Wine
The Hess Collection
The Ordinary Fellow & Dry Storage
The Original Ninfa's
The Pale Rosé by Sacha Lichine
The Sorting Table
Tip Top Proper Cocktails
Tom Beckbe
Tribute Wines
TRUFF
Truffle Shuffle
Uncle Nearest Premium Whiskey
Viña TerraNoble
Vineyard Brands
Vintage Point
Vintage Wine Estates
Vivanterre
Volio Imports
Voyage Foods
Westward Whiskey
White Claw Hard Seltzer
Wine Chips
Wines of Chile
Woody Creek Distillers

Join us next year for the 39th FOOD & WINE Classic In Aspen, June 17-19, 2022!
CLASSIC.FOODANDWINE.COM

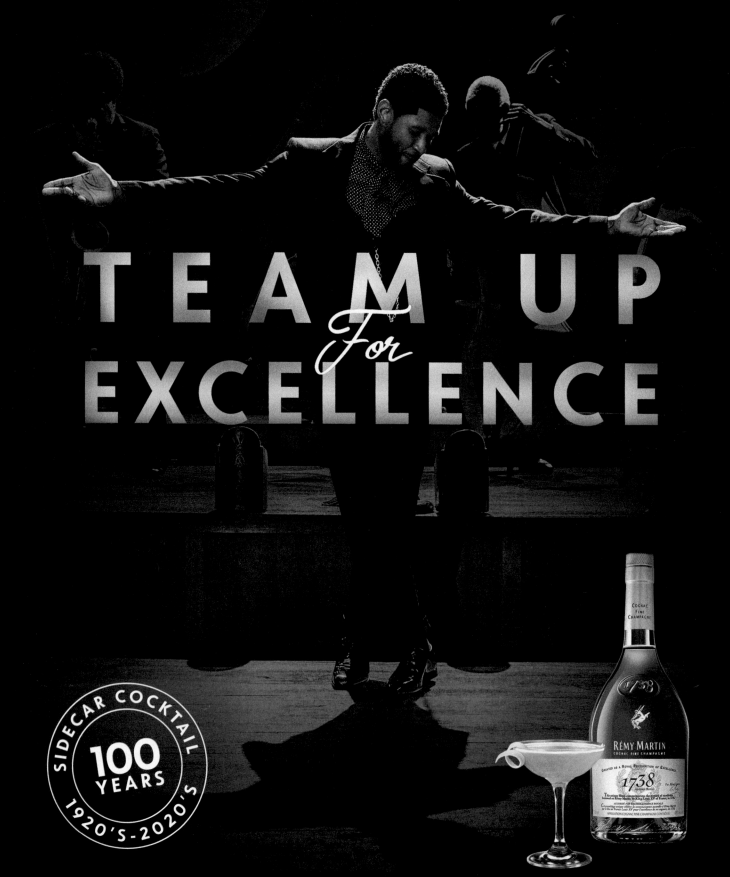

TRAVEL

WHERE TO GO NEXT

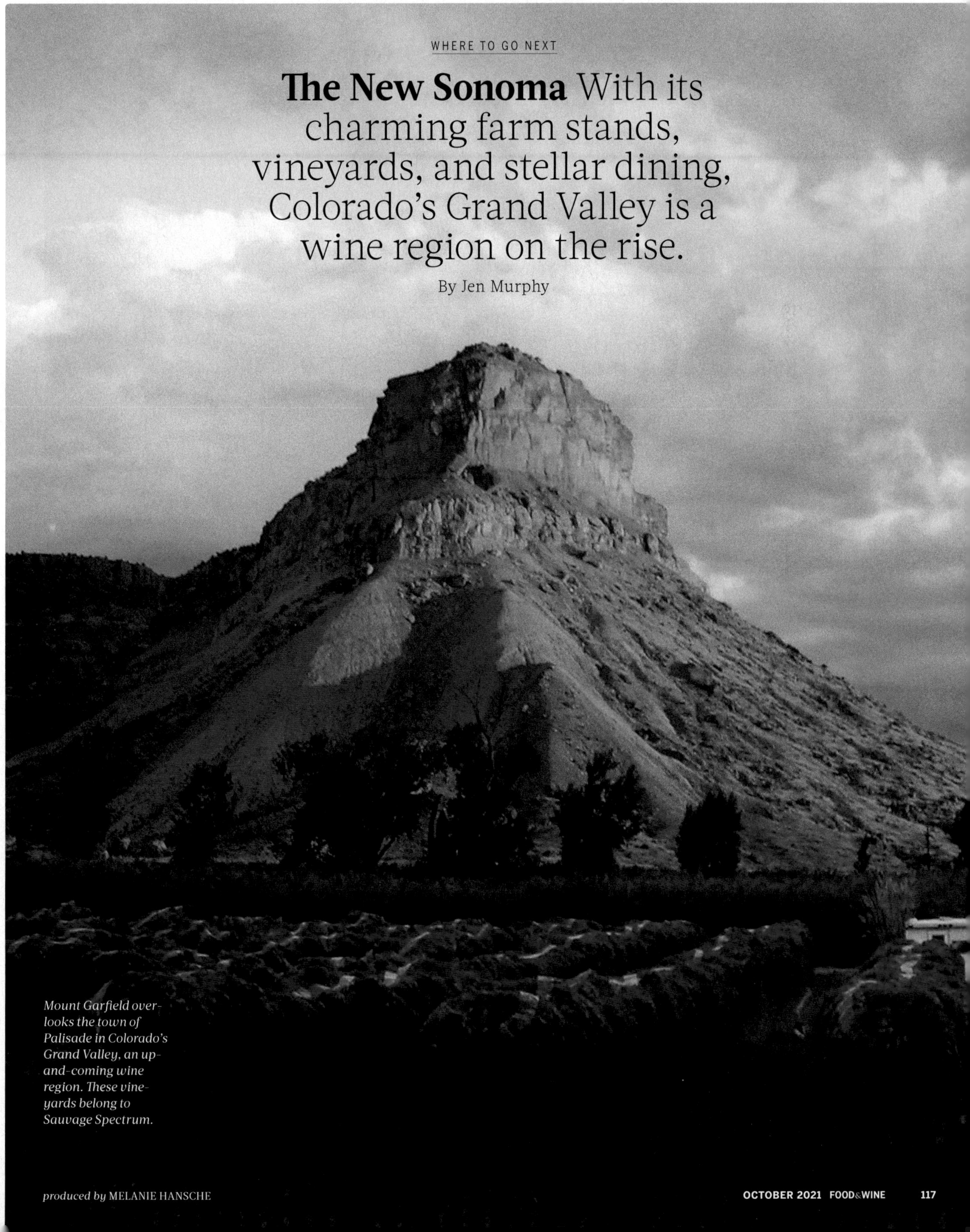

The New Sonoma With its charming farm stands, vineyards, and stellar dining, Colorado's Grand Valley is a wine region on the rise.

By Jen Murphy

Mount Garfield overlooks the town of Palisade in Colorado's Grand Valley, an up-and-coming wine region. These vineyards belong to Sauvage Spectrum.

PHOTOGRAPHY: COURTESY OF SAUVAGE SPECTRUM

produced by MELANIE HANSCHE

WHEN I MOVED from the Bay Area to Colorado five years ago, a road trip through the state's wine country wasn't on my to-do list. Spoiled from having Napa and Sonoma in my backyard, I turned my nose up at the idea of Colorado wines and focused on what the state was best known for: skiing, hiking, biking, and beer. But last year, with travel limited due to the pandemic, I finally explored my new home state with an open mind.

Grand Valley, on Colorado's Western Slope, about four hours west of Denver, is an agricultural mecca. And it turns out that the sunny days and cool nights responsible for the region's famous peaches are also ideal conditions for growing grapes, particularly quicker-to-ripen, high-elevation varietals like Viognier, Riesling, and Mourvèdre. Dotted with unpretentious tasting rooms, mom-and-pop fruit stands, and family-run farms, it transported me to Sonoma's Russian River Valley, but with rocky mesas rather than redwoods.

In recent years, a handful of ambitious chefs and winemakers have helped turn the Grand Valley region, which includes the towns of Palisade, Grand Junction, and Fruita, into a legitimate culinary destination. Colorado native and 2020 James Beard Award semifinalist Josh Niernberg was one of the first chefs to spotlight the area's bounty when he opened Bin 707 Foodbar in Grand Junction a decade ago. "This is Colorado's breadbasket," he says. "It's an area rich with agricultural history."

Niernberg's New West cuisine is infused with high-desert flavors like guajillo peppers, sagebrush, and juniper berries, and dishes such as Colorado mayocoba bean cassoulet with cornmeal fried rabbit are a nod to the area's Mexican and European immigrants. Wanting to support the local wine scene, Niernberg recently began collaborating with one of Colorado's oldest wineries, Carlson Vineyards, located in nearby Palisade, to create house whites and reds under the High Desert Wine Lab label.

Over a long weekend, I quickly caught on that the best way to experience Grand Valley's vineyards and orchards is by bike. Jody Corey and Jeff Snook, owners of Palisade's

Hotel Maverick's terrace (ABOVE) offers stellar sunset views over Grand Junction and the Grand Mesa, while its lobby and lounge (BELOW) offer cozy corners, couches, and a fireplace.

WHERE TO STAY

SPOKE AND VINE MOTEL

The food- and cycling-obsessed owners of this 1950s motor lodge–turned–18-room boutique stay in Palisade are happy to stock your mini fridge in advance with locavore snack boards curated by Taste of Palisade. *(Rooms from $159, spoke andvinemotel.com)*

HOTEL MAVERICK

This year-old property is Grand Junction's first boutique stay and has 60 mountain-modern rooms. The rooftop restaurant pairs comforting fare like elk burgers and fried chicken sammies with some of the best views of the Grand Mesa and Colorado National Monument. *(Rooms from $209, thehotelmaverick.com)*

ONCE YOU KNOW, YOU'LL

never forget

HILTON HEAD ISLAND
SOUTH CAROLINA

Follow the path to America's Favorite Island®.
32.2163° N, 80.7526° W

HiltonHeadIsland.org

hip new Spoke and Vine Motel, are the ultimate hosts, directing guests to their favorite single-track rides, tasting rooms, and restaurants. The hotel rents out cruiser bikes kitted out with baskets to hold the treats you're certain to purchase on a tasting tour of the East Orchard Mesa Loop. On this 25-mile path, riders pass a dozen wineries (including Carlson), plus farm stands like Anita's Pantry and Produce and Aloha Organic Fruit, all while taking in stunning views of the towering Grand Mesa, the world's largest flat-top mountain.

You'll be glad you pedaled up an appetite if you've been lucky enough to score a table at Pêche. One of Colorado's most exciting restaurants, Pêche combines five-star service with a welcoming, easygoing atmosphere. Chef Matt Chasseur and his wife, Ashley Fees Chasseur, both alumni of Chicago's modernist restaurant Alinea, like to say that they discovered Palisade by accident. Matt was working at a ranch 30 minutes away and realized he was doing all of his personal grocery shopping at farm stands in Palisade. "I was blown away not just by the quality of the products but by the drive and dedication of the people making them," he says. When a restaurant space became available in town, the couple scooped it up with the goal of creating a space where locals could be spoiled with hospitality and delicious food.

A celebration of Grand Valley artisans, the menu lets local ingredients shine; in peak growing season, Matt can source most everything–even wines and spirits–from within a two-mile radius. That local devotion has resonated with the community, many of whom keep weekly standing reservations.

Unable to restrain myself from the chewy sourdough served with creamy cultured butter from Ghost Rock Farm, I found myself asking to take dessert home. On learning I was staying at the Spoke and Vine, Matt happily presented my lemon meringue with lady fingers in a glass dish with a metal spoon, and asked me to have Jody and Jeff return the dishes when they dined there later that week. Now that's community hospitality.

Chef Josh Niernberg's restaurant Bin 707 Foodbar features a dessert pie menu, including this panna cotta pie with blood orange sauce (BELOW). The menu at his more casual Taco Party features vibrant Mexican-inspired dishes made with 100% local produce (BOTTOM).

WHERE TO EAT

PÊCHE

Opened in August 2019 by two Alinea alumni, Pêche has put Palisade on the destination dining map with its hyper-seasonal fine-dining menu and laid-back vibe. *(peche restaurantcolorado.com)*

TACO PARTY

The casual sister to Bin 707 Foodbar focuses on inventive tacos (hot fried chicken with huitlacoche aioli), riffs on Southwestern staples (duck liver mousse tostadas), and seasonal soft serve in flavors like white chocolate and corn. *(tacopartygj.com)*

BIN 707 FOODBAR

The pioneer of Colorado's farm-to-table scene features dishes designed around high-desert flavors paired with Grand Valley wines and cocktails crafted with regional spirits. *(bin707.com)*

HANDLEBAR TAP HOUSE

A location near popular bike trails and a menu of craft beers and creative burgers make this Grand Junction spot a favorite haunt of local cyclists. *(handlebargj.com)*

WHERE TO DRINK

PRESSED

Serves locally roasted coffee infused with CBD from the owner's hemp farm by day and craft cocktails at night. *(pressedinpalisade.com)*

CARLSON VINEYARDS

Known for its Rieslings and Gewürztraminers, Carlson also produces wines like the juicy, vibrant Exodus Blaufränkisch under its High Desert Wine Lab label, a collaboration with the chef at Bin 707 Foodbar. *(carlsonvineyards.com)*

THE STORM CELLAR

At 5,880 feet, this is one of the highest-elevation vineyards in the Northern Hemisphere, located in nearby Hotchkiss. It's earned accolades for producing crisp, acidic whites like its dry Riesling. A tasting room debuted this summer. *(stormcellarwine.com)*

SAUVAGE SPECTRUM

This Palisade newcomer already has a following for its fruit-forward, easy-drinking reds and pét-nats. *(sauvagespectrum .com)*

RAMBLEBINE BREWING COMPANY

This new downtown taproom in Grand Junction features more than a dozen beers, including seasonal sours and farmhouse ales. *(ramblebine brewing.com)*

COLORADO MOUNTAIN WINEFEST

Held every September in Palisade, this festival is the place to get schooled on the state's wine scene. *(coloradowinefest.com)*

The distinctively rocky Mount Garfield is part of the Book Cliffs range on Colorado's Western Slope. It is mesmerizing in the winter, when vines at Carlson Vineyards lie dormant, but the surrounding towns are still humming with excellent drinking and dining.

you'll always

FIND YOUR WAY BACK

HILTON HEAD ISLAND
SOUTH CAROLINA

America's Favorite Island®.
32.2163° N, 80.7526° W

HiltonHeadIsland.org

GREY GOOSE®
ESSENCES

THE TASTE OF FRESH FRUIT AND BOTANICAL ESSENCES.
ONLY 73 CALORIES.

Meet the 2021 Class of

BEST NEW CHIEFS

BY KHUSHBU SHAH

PHOTOGRAPHY BY CEDRIC ANGELES

I don't know how restaurants work anymore.

I've come to this conclusion after spending the spring traversing the country (fully vaccinated) and eating in as many cities as I possibly could (fewer than usual, due to the circumstances). Everything was different; even fine dining was to-go. Menus were accessed by QR codes, and it was weeks before I encountered a real plate. But it's not just the experience of dining that's different (for more on that, see "The New Rules of Dining Out," p. 46); what it means to be a chef has changed.

This is an industry that was built on a shaky foundation, and the global pandemic put a spotlight on every single crack. But through these cracks, real leadership emerged. Leadership that prioritizes the safety and needs of employees over the whims of customers. Leadership that centers local communities, providing groceries and hot meals for those in need. Leadership that still turns out exceptional cooking that manages to comfort and delight even when the odds are stacked against them.

This year's class of Best New Chefs exemplifies this approach to leadership. There's the chef in Austin who is running an ambitious in-house masa program while prioritizing the mental health of his team, and the pastry chef in Washington, D.C., who is baking whimsical desserts that center the flavors of her Dominican heritage while launching bake sales that help combat racism. There's the scrappy chef in Portland, Oregon, who is making America fall in love with the robust and complex flavors of Filipino food and building a gathering space for his community, and the chef in Ann Arbor, Michigan, who merges Midwestern produce with centuries-old Korean recipes while also compensating her staff well above market standards and providing a slew of benefits.

From coast to coast, the 2021 class of Best New Chefs is reinventing what it means to lead in the kitchen while cooking the food that matters to them most. Restaurants may no longer look the same, but with this class of chefs at the helm, I am excited to see—and eat—what the future holds. **—KHUSHBU SHAH**

Where do *Food & Wine* Best New Chefs like to eat, drink, and shop when they're not at their own restaurants? In the pages that follow, this year's class of Best New Chefs shouts out their favorite eateries, bars, and other must-visit destinations for food lovers in the cities they call home. **CITY GUIDES PRODUCED BY MELANIE HANSCHE & NINA FRIEND**

Matt Horn

HORN BARBECUE, OAKLAND, CALIFORNIA

THIS SELF-TAUGHT PITMASTER, WHO HAS NEVER WORKED IN ANY RESTAURANT BUT HIS OWN, DIDN'T START COOKING UNTIL HIS TWENTIES. TODAY, HE'S MAKING UP FOR LOST TIME WITH A SINGLE-MINDED DEDICATION AND A UNIQUE, PERSONAL, AND DELICIOUS STYLE OF BARBECUE.

PHOTOGRAPHY BY AUBRIE PICK

MATT'S OAKLAND CITY GUIDE

IN THE CRACKLING FLAMES of the fire he had just lit in his grandmother's backyard, Matt Horn found his life's calling. "The smoke is in your face; you're hearing the wood cracking; you're seeing the embers," he says. "It was transformative. I zoned out. Nothing else around me mattered." That was it—he was hooked. Horn knew at that moment that he would spend his life pursuing the mastery of barbecue.

Horn's apartment complex in Inglewood, California, wouldn't allow him to set up a fire, but his grandmother, who lives in Fresno, still had his grandfather's barbecue firepit intact. It was once used for family gatherings but had sat dormant for over a decade. There, Horn became a self-taught student of barbecue. He experimented with various woods, cooking times, and temperatures, tracking his findings in a notebook. He slept outside so he could monitor the flames. Horn chose to teach himself instead of working for someone because he wanted to develop his own style: "I didn't want to learn anyone else's method," he says.

Shortly after this, Horn, his wife, Nina, and their infant son moved in with his in-laws in Tracy, California. A week after his first visit to the local farmers market, he decided to start selling his barbecue there. He had just eight customers on the first day, but he was still over the moon. "It was an opportunity for me to put my product out there, to get feedback from people that weren't family—and people loved it."

Horn set his sights on doing pop-ups. During his first, he didn't sell a single plate of food. He almost gave up, but that night he dreamed he was looking out of a building, seeing people lined up down the block for his food. He awoke recommitted to his vision and reached out to 40 different businesses in the Bay Area to see if they could host a pop-up. That led him to the permanent space where he now cooks out of a 1,000-gallon offset smoker (a real upgrade from a backyard firepit).

At Horn's, customers wait for hours for his brisket, cooked low and slow for 16 to 18 hours and sliced to order. It's a transcendent mouthful: the bark charred, the meat moist, and the fat so wobbly it gently coats your tongue. They're also drawn to the housemade hot links, plump and bursting with spicy meat, and the smoked turkey breast, flavorful and tender even without the use of a brine. It's worth saving room for the cheesy potato casserole. In an ode to his grandmother, Horn bakes little cubes of potatoes with cream of chicken soup, sour cream, butter, and cheddar cheese. For dessert, Nina makes trays of creamy banana pudding.

Horn's approach to barbecue is hard to fit in a box. "When I cook barbecue, I look at it and I'm like, 'How can I turn this raw piece of meat into something that's a work of art?' That's how I look at the barbecue that I do. But also, I want it to tell a story," explains Horn. He is on a mission to pay homage to the Black pitmasters, well-known and forgotten, who paved the way.

Horn is only just getting started. He is about to open Kowbird, a Southern-style fried chicken restaurant, and, later this year, a burger concept called Matty's Old Fashioned and a trailer that will serve tacos and smoked meat. "I don't like doing anything halfway," says Horn. "I feel like time is life's most precious commodity, and I don't like to waste it at all."

A spread at Horn Barbecue, including brisket, beef ribs, turkey, and spare ribs. Collards, mac and cheese, and a variety of pickles that help cut through the smoke and fat play important supporting roles. The beef ribs are a Saturday special; the turkey is only on the menu on Sundays. Don't forget to leave room for the banana pudding made by Horn's wife, Nina.

FEED YOUR SOUL
"Minnie Bell's Soul Movement (minnie bellssoul.com) has some delicious, authentic food. Chef Fernay McPherson's menu isn't expansive, and that's what I like about it. She has a limited selection, all executed well and with passion. Her dishes are home-style, mainly made from family recipes that were passed down and are rooted in tradition, so you can feel the love and warmth poured into each one. My go-to order is the signature rosemary fried chicken, braised collard greens, and mac and cheese."

GOOD VIBES
"For a fancy night out, I start at chef Nelson German's seafood spot, alaMar Kitchen & Bar (alamaroakland.com). I order the garlic udon noodles, served with a fried egg on top, and head-on Cajun shrimp. After dinner, I would head over to Bar Shiru (barshiru.com) in Uptown Oakland. They have a cool musical vibe, playing only hi-fi vinyl records, and a top-notch drink selection. I recommend the Kurayoshi 18 whiskey; it's super smooth and pairs perfectly with the overall ambience of the space."

CAFFEINE RUSH
"My wife, Nina, and I love the Vietnamese coffee from Orbit Coffee (orbit.coffee)."

BREAD AHEAD
"Firebrand Artisan Breads (firebrand bread.com) uses simple but high-quality ingredients, and the loaves have that perfect crunchy, scored crust and soft, slightly tangy interior."

FINE WINE
"Ordinaire (ordinaire wine.com) is my favorite wine shop. They have a large selection of California wines, and it's a great spot to discover small, local winemakers."

THE PLACE TO BE
"My family and I like to walk around Grand Lake Farmers Market (agriculturalinstitute .org) at Lake Merritt to pick up fresh, high-quality produce and picnic on the lake. It's the place to be on the weekend."

PURE EGGCELLENCE
"I like a good brunch on the weekend, and it doesn't get much better than the smoked salmon soft scramble at Limewood Bar & Restaurant (limewood restaurant.com) [located inside the Claremont Club & Spa]."

LIMITED EDITION
"When I need to buy a gift, I head over to Alkali Rye (sipalkali rye.com) and grab a bottle of small-batch bourbon or whiskey. They have a great selection of top-quality, limited-run spirits."

Paola Velez

WASHINGTON, D.C.

THIS JOYFUL PASTRY CHEF'S BOLD AND VIBRANT DESSERTS ARE MATCHED BY HER ENERGY, HUMOR, AND ENTHUSIASM TO IMPROVE KITCHEN CULTURE AND HELP MAKE THE HOSPITALITY INDUSTRY A MORE FAIR AND EQUITABLE PLACE.

PHOTOGRAPHY BY ALEX LAU

THE PIÑA COLADA DOUGHNUT from La Bodega is a feat of pastry engineering. It's about as large as the head of an infant, but the brioche remains improbably light for something that has been deep-fried. Its architect, pastry chef Paola Velez, wanted to create a dessert that made her feel like she was "at the Dole factory in Hawaii," so the doughnut is blanketed in an intense pineapple glaze that's a pinch salty and slightly acidic thanks to lime juice and citric acid. The doughnut itself is sweet, but not overly so, with a gentle vanilla-bean cascade that lingers after each bite. To bring it all together, Velez stuffs each one with a pillow's worth of lush coconut-and-rum-infused pastry cream.

Velez's pastry creations–which include thick sticky buns rippled with pureed sweet plantain, hefty cookies she calls "thick'ems" packed with white chocolate chunks, and bright pink strawberry knafeh piled high with phyllo shards–are unapologetic in their size and flavor. They refuse to be background notes or secondary to a meal. They are not subtle. They are not fragile. They are celebratory expressions of technique and culture. They are like Velez.

"I just want people to get the most out of the desserts they possibly can," she says. The brilliance and boldness of her vision in the kitchen is matched by her commitment to using her success to help others. Over the past two years, while earning several accolades for her pastries, Velez has emerged as one of the most vocal and trusted chefs in the industry, speaking out against toxic kitchen culture, racism, wage disparity, and the lack of equity in the culinary world. Velez speaks about these subjects candidly and manages to do it all through a lens of positivity, constantly shouting out peers in the industry, working in moments of playful humor (just check out her TikTok account), and focusing on moments of joy.

Velez grew up in the Bronx and was hooked on the idea of being a chef at a young age, attending Le Cordon Bleu in Orlando. Afterward, she moved back to New York, where she struggled to find steady work that she loved. That changed after she convinced legendary chocolatier Jacques Torres to hire her, working her way up to a pastry sous position within four months. But no sooner had she found her footing than her husband's job moved them to Washington, D.C., where she had to start over from scratch. She eventually landed at Iron Gate, where she ran the pastry kitchen, before Kwame Onwuachi (2019 F&W Best New Chef) invited her to run the pastry program at Kith/Kin, where she showcased the flavors of her Dominican heritage.

TOP LEFT: Soursop–olive oil torta with passion fruit Italian buttercream. TOP RIGHT: Velez's signature nutmeg-spiced brioche doughnuts with vanilla icing. BOTTOM LEFT: Velez with Nikkie Rodriguez (middle) and DeAndra Bailey (left), two pastry cooks from La Bodega (currently on hiatus). BOTTOM RIGHT: A rainbow opera cake, made in celebration of Pride Month.

Then, the pandemic hit. Suddenly furloughed, she turned to activism. Velez launched a doughnut pop-up, Doña Dona, to raise funds for undocumented restaurant workers and co-founded Bakers Against Racism, followed by a stint as the pastry chef at D.C. restaurants Compass Rose and Maydan, while also running La Bodega, her now-on-hiatus desserts pop-up. (Follow her on Instagram @smallorchids for where to find her pastries next.) Velez has found her voice, and she is determined to leave the industry better than she found it. "I hope that other people feel that they can be exactly who they are," she says. "That others are inspired to do what I'm doing, so I'm not the only one."

NATTY WINE

"My husband and I absolutely love natural wine—whether it's a bottle of Scotty-Boy! blush, Gaia Assyrtiko Wild Ferment, or something a bit more funky and obscure, we're always down to try it! Our go-to shop in D.C. is **Domestique** (*domestiquewine.com*), a wine shop dedicated to natural wines."

COCKTAIL HOUR

"I really like Dark and Stormys, but the ginger beer needs to be fresh and spicy and not overly sweet. My cocktail spot is **Serenata** (*serenatadc .com*). Beverage director and partner Andra 'AJ' Johnson is a maven behind the bar, making amazing drinks that have garnered nationwide recognition."

PEACE AND QUIET

"**Little Pearl** (*little pearldc.com*) is a lovely little wine bar in Capitol Hill with a killer wine list and tasty bites. Even though they are only one block away from the main strip on Barracks Row, sitting on their patio feels like you've been transported miles away from the bustle of the city."

BEST BITES

"**Albi** (*albidc.com*) is chef Michael Rafidi's love letter to Levantine cuisine. Think fire-roasted meats and pitas, flavorful savory spreads, and seasonal veggies. Dinner is best shared, allowing you to order more plates than you should without garnering the judgmental gaze of fellow diners at the next table. (Pro tip: Don't leave without trying the labneh soft serve!) **Moon Rabbit** (*moonrabbitdc .com*) is always a fun experience! From their impossibly crispy take on the Filet-O-Fish to a Hi-Chew green melon cocktail that has me absolutely hooked, I'm consistently and constantly blown away."

RAD GIFTS

"My go-to shop for gifts in D.C. is **Hill's Kitchen** (*hillskitchen.com*). Not only is it a woman-owned small business, but they have a great selection of kitchen tools, cookbooks, and culinary knickknacks. The owner, Leah, is super helpful and rad!"

HIDDEN GEM

"**Jam Doung Style** (*jamdoungstyle.com*) is an amazing, local, Black-owned spot that serves the best, most authentic Jamaican food in D.C. Being introduced to Jam Doung is like falling into the arms of your favorite aunt after not seeing her for a while—pure comfort. My go-to dish is the oxtail plate, with rice and peas (with extra brown stew sauce on top), cabbage, mac and cheese, and sweet plantain. And don't forget the beef patty!"

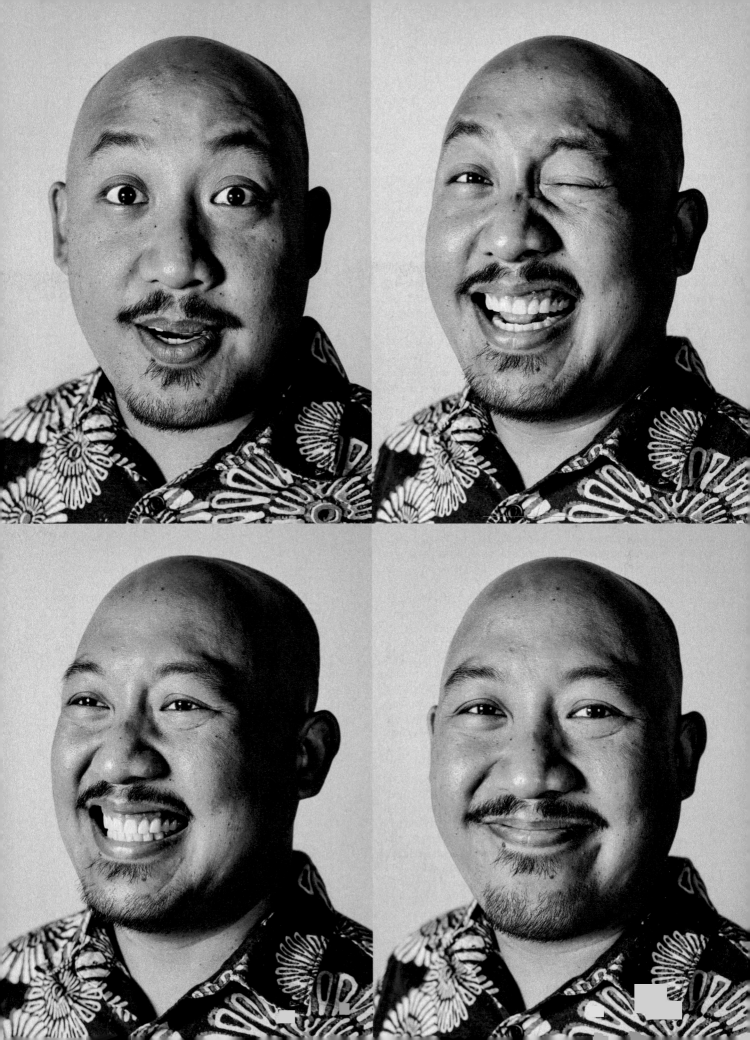

Carlo Lamagna

MAGNA KUSINA, PORTLAND, OREGON

FAMILY IS CENTRAL TO THIS FILIPINO CHEF'S FOOD AND PHILOSOPHY. HIS COOKING IS AN HOMAGE TO THE VIBRANT FLAVORS OF HIS CHILDHOOD, A TRIBUTE TO HIS LATE FATHER, AND A PROMISE TO A COMMUNITY WHOSE AMBITIONS HE WANTS TO SUPPORT.

PHOTOGRAPHY BY AUBRIE PICK

CARLO LAMAGNA APPROACHES Filipino food like a Grand Prix race car driver: He drives with extreme precision and finesse, but he isn't afraid to press on the gas. The translucent broth that forms the base of the sinigang at Magna Kusina, Lamagna's Portland, Oregon, restaurant, has the elegant gleam of consommé but is anything but subtle in flavor. It fully embraces its sour notes, with punches of tamarind knitted together by tomato, fish stock and fish sauce, onions, and garlic. And then there's the electrifying, elemental funk that ripples through the bagoong alamang, a condiment of fermented shrimp paste spiked with garlic, fish sauce, and palm sugar. It's a favorite childhood food of Lamagna's, given a cheffy makeover in a dish called mangga at bagoong alamang: It arrives at the table in a small boat carved out of raw green mango and is covered with a shower of edible flower petals.

To walk into Magna Kusina is to walk into a dinner party at Lamagna's house. The dining room radiates welcoming warmth. There are heavy pours of Oregon wines, and Janet Jackson plays over the sound system. Lamagna feeds you with the joy of an auntie who hasn't seen you in decades, passing you generous portions of pancit miki-bihon, bulked up with a combination of rice noodles and housemade egg noodles,

BELOW: A kamayan dinner at Magna Kusina includes rice, lumpia, grilled shrimp, seasonal vegetables, mussels, shrimp chips, and Dungeness crab served on banana leaves. OPPOSITE, TOP: Lamagna (far right) and his family and team at Magna Kusina. OPPO-SITE, BOTTOM: Sisig, crispy pork marinated in soy sauce and cala-mansi, topped with a fried egg and chiles.

and meaty, crispy lumpia packed with pork and mushrooms and fried.

For Lamagna, Magna is more than a place to champion Filipino cooking. It's also a way to honor his late father. "One of the last things he said to me was, 'I'm proud of you. I am not worried about you. Just promise me you won't forget who you are and where you come from.'" It's a promise Lamagna knew he could keep through food. "From the point that he passed away to now, the goal was to open a Filipino restaurant and show the world our family's culture," he says.

Lamagna was born in the Philippines but spent a large part of his childhood in Detroit, returning to the Philippines when he was 11 and staying through high school and college. After getting kicked out of college, Lamagna made his way back to Detroit, where he attended a local culinary program while working at a slew of restaurants across the city, from a country club to a sushi bar.

After that, he decided it was time to take his career seriously, enrolling at the Culinary Institute of America. After graduating, he landed a job in Chicago, where he eventually worked for chef Paul Virant. An opportunity in the kitchen at Clyde Common brought Lamagna to Portland. He was laid off after nearly three and a half years there, and he decided it was time to stop working for other people and to chase his dream of opening his own Filipino spot. He did pop-up dinners for two years before Magna Kusina opened in August 2019.

Long term, Lamagna dreams that Magna will one day become a pillar in the Filipino community. "I want it to be more than just a restaurant," Lamagna says. "I want it to be a place where people feel safe and comfortable, and where they can come together and share stories." He imagines Magna as a communal space, where others can launch their own ideas and pop-ups. And he hopes it will one day be a restaurant that "turns out some amazing chefs in their own right."

As for that last point, he is well on his way: Most of the people who work for Lamagna have been with him for at least two years, with one of his sous chefs coming up on 11 years of working together. "Ultimately, I just want to be able to have something that my kids are proud to say, 'Hey, look. This is what my dad did,'" says Lamagna. "The same way that I talk about my dad, I want them to talk about me."

CARLO'S PORTLAND CITY GUIDE

PORTLAND PROUD

"The food-cart scene here is pretty epic, and I would consider it a defining quality of Portland. Places like **Kim Jong Grillin** (*kjgpdx .com*), a Korean food cart; **Matta** (*mattapdx .com*), which serves Vietnamese; and **Bing Mi** (*bingmiportland .com*), a Chinese pancake place, are quite representative of the amazing food carts that show off the many different foods the city has to offer."

SECRET SPOT

"There are so many unique experiences around town, but one in particular that stands out is an underground backyard dinner experience at **JEM by Joel and Emily Stocks** (*thestockshouse.com*). Joel is an amazing chef, born and raised in Portland, and brings his fine-dining experience to his garage, which he has turned into a dining space. It's a unique, interactive experience, from cocktails in their backyard garden to a multicourse dinner paired with amazing wines, all executed at a high level you could expect in any fine-dining restaurant."

SIMPLE PLEASURES

"I am a simple guy and love greasy spoons! My go-to dish is corned beef hash with solid hash browns. I hit up **Dockside Saloon** (*docksidesaloon.com*) when I am craving it. Their hash browns are probably the best in the city."

WINES OF OREGON

"**Les Caves** (*lescaves pdx.com*) is my go-to wine bar. I completely trust [co-owner and winemaker] Jeff Vejr and his selection of wines, as well as his own label, Golden Cluster. They make some amazing wines representative of Oregon and showcasing the expansive repertoire we have to offer, not just Pinot Noir."

PRIZE PASTRY

"The mushroom tart at **JinJu Patisserie** (*jinju patisserie.com*) is one of the best pastries in this city, if not the country. I guess that's what happens when you team a master chocolatier (Jin Caldwell) with a pastry chef (Kyurim Lee) who trained with some of the best in the craft under one roof. Honestly, everything at that shop is amazing."

FEEL-GOOD PIZZA

"Chef Shardell Dues from **Red Sauce Pizza** (*redsaucepizza.com*) is a badass when it comes to slinging pizza. She supports local farms and is a pillar in the community. My go-to pizzas are the Hot Nancy, with ricotta, red onion, hot honey, and sea salt, and the Princess Sarah, with sausage and house-pickled peppers."

Thessa Diadem

ALL DAY BABY, LOS ANGELES

THIS BEST NEW CHEF DRAWS INSPIRATION FROM THE INTERNATIONAL GROCERY STORES OF LOS ANGELES AND CHANNELS THEM INTO HER INNOVATIVE, DECADENT PASTRIES—FROM A CUSTARDY UBE PIE TO FLUFFY, TENDER CONCHAS.

PHOTOGRAPHY BY AUBRIE PICK

COOK THE COVER

GET THE RECIPE AT FOODANDWINE.COM/SWEET-POTATO-STICKY-BUNS.

LIKE A LOCAL

THESSA'S L.A. CITY GUIDE

▶

BEST CUPPA

"I love the Stockholm Fog, a mix of mocha and chai, at my favorite coffee shop, **The Boy & The Bear** (*theboyand thebear.com*) in Culver City. You can get it hot or cold, but the move is to get it with an extra shot of espresso!"

CARB CITY

"Andy Kadin of **Bub and Grandma's Bread** (*bubandgrandmas .com*) makes the best loaves in Los Angeles. My freezer was stocked with his incredible sesame sourdough loaf when quarantine started."

THEY SAY THAT YOU EAT WITH YOUR EYES first, and it's impossible to not have yours widen with hunger when you spot slices of chef Thessa Diadem's velvety ube pie in the pastry case at All Day Baby in Los Angeles. The thick ube custard, a shade of purple so saturated and vivid that Prince might have been jealous, sits up in an impossibly flaky crust. Each piece is topped with a cascade of chamomile-spiked whipped cream puffs that gather like clouds before a rainstorm.

Yes, the ube pie is a nod to Diadem's Filipina heritage (she immigrated to the United States at the age of 13), but it also represents her broader approach in the kitchen: using the most global flavors that she can source locally. She finds her inspiration in the international grocery stores around All Day Baby, where Diadem heads up the pastry program. "I love finding things that I've never worked with to play around with," she says. While walking around Mercado Benito Juarez in L.A.'s Koreatown, she became enraptured with a pile of avocado leaves. "They smell and taste like anise," she says. Diadem bought as many as she could, transforming the leaves into a galette for an intricate, multipart plated dessert with a sorrel granita and espuma made from a Georgian pear soda. She regularly purchases 10-pound batches of halvah, which become chewy cookies studded with chocolate and walnuts. She is currently figuring out what to do with her stash of eucalyptus and fermented black nuts from the Indonesian market.

As a teen, Diadem had no ideas about her future. After high school, at her father's urging, she moved to New York City to study at what is now ICE, the Institute of Culinary Education. "At first I was just doing it because I wanted my dad off my back, but on my first day, I just realized this is where I was supposed to be," Diadem recalls. But she found living on a cook's salary in New York impossible, and she moved back to Los Angeles to work at a hotel operation. That led to a stint at Mezze (now shuttered) and a job as the pastry chef for restaurateurs Jon Shook and Vinny Dotolo.

For Diadem, having a career suddenly take off was a blessing and a curse. At 28, she felt burned out. She flew to Italy and spent six months gathering herself, all the while receiving a stream of messages from chef Jonathan

AT RIGHT: Diadem's team is responsible for over 1,000 biscuits each week. They're the foundation of the ADB Biscuit Sandwich, enveloping scrambled eggs, cheese, strawberry jam, bacon, and sausage. OPPOSITE: A sweet potato sticky bun at All Day Baby, filled with spiced sweet potato, drizzled in cinnamon butterscotch, and topped with toasted marshmallow.

Whitener, her former coworker, asking her to sign on at his new concepts, All Day Baby and Here's Looking at You. She agreed to return after her Italian visa ran out–which gave her one week to create the opening dessert menu for Here's Looking at You (which closed during the pandemic). Diadem, who talks openly about her struggles with anxiety, admits that it was nerve-racking but also exhilarating: This was the first time in her career she had full control over the menu.

All Day Baby is a high-volume operation, but Diadem is a calm and gentle presence, shaped by years of observing how she didn't want to be in a kitchen. "In my day, you worked for free or off the clock because you placed so much importance in the job you wanted to keep," she says. The lack of boundaries took a toll on her health, she says. "It's exploitation disguising itself as passion." Diadem eventually learned how to say "no" more often and taught herself to meditate. She is optimistic about the future of the restaurant industry, as long as it is rooted in self-care, and hopes more people won't have to learn the lessons the hard way, as she did: "I think it's really critical for restaurants and employers to honor the value of their employees and show them that their time is appreciated."

BEST BRUNCH
"I love to brunch at **Destroyer** (destroyer .la). I'm obsessed with the bowl of fresh blueberries with black currants, lime, and elderflower. The beef tartare and mushroom-Gruyère croissant are also unmissable."

THE DINNER MOVE
"Head with friends you adore to **Chi Spacca** (chispacca.com). Start with the affettati misti and the anchovies and butter. Get the roasted cauliflower, the prawns, and the porterhouse, plus a bottle of red. End the night with gelato."

WINE TIME
"**Vinovore** (vinovore .com) features women winemakers from all over the world. The bottles all have handwritten labels listing the name of the winemaker, grape varietal, and fun descriptions of the wine's flavor profile."

DESTINATION CHEESE
"The cheese course from **Scratch | Bar & Kitchen's** tasting menu (scratchrestaurants .com) is a pat of triple-crème cheese ice cream with a slice of toasted brioche. It bridges to the dessert course perfectly."

SIP BACK & RELAX
"**Oriel** (orielchinatown .com) in Chinatown is one of my favorite wine bars. It has a list of exceptional wines and food to match. Get the cheese-and-charcuterie board, escargot, and the duck in a jar to enjoy with your wine."

GROCERY LIST
"I'm inspired by Mercado Benito Juarez, Silom Supermarket, Galleria Market, 99 Ranch, A&S Market, and India Food Mart, just to name a few. The Silver Lake Farmers Market is sweet—good for a quick haul."

Fermín Núñez

SUERTE, AUSTIN

AT HIS GROUNDBREAKING RESTAURANT, THIS CHEF IS ADVANCING A NEW DEFINITION OF TEX-MEX COOKING THROUGH FRESH MASA, "BLACK MAGIC OIL," AND THE GOSPEL OF GREAT TORTILLAS.

PHOTOGRAPHY BY CEDRIC ANGELES

YOU CAN SMELL SUERTE from a block away. East Sixth Street is one of Austin's busiest thoroughfares, but follow the unmistakable aroma of toasted corn and you will find yourself standing in front of chef Fermín Núñez's altar to all things masa. It's devoted to the art of nixtamalization, a process that prepares dried corn kernels to be ground into the fresh dough used to make tortillas and tostadas so redolent with flavor that they will have you asking if you've ever truly tasted corn before.

Núñez partners with Barton Springs Mill, which works with local farmers around Texas, to source the highest-quality corn possible. He is extremely proud of the result. "Our tortillas, they're not like Mexican tortillas," he says. "But they are inspired by Mexico, and they taste to me like Mexico." The busiest station in the kitchen is the tortilla station, which produces between 2,500 and 3,000 from-scratch tortillas each shift. It is typically operated by one person.

Ultimately, Núñez's goal with the food at Suerte is to give it a real sense of place, while honoring his roots as a Mexican immigrant. "Suerte is its own little Mexico, but in Austin," he explains. "Its first language is English, but it's fluent in Spanish." It's a philosophy he has expanded to other parts of the menu.

Take the tender suadero tacos on every table: Núñez and his team combine slow-cooked brisket with what he calls "black magic oil," a mixture of toasted garlic, morita chiles, and black sesame seeds. It's also evident in the rotating selection of crudos, aguachiles, and ceviches (served with the restaurant's excellent tostadas). Fresh fish is seasoned

BELOW, CLOCKWISE FROM MIDDLE: Suerte Ceviche with Juliet tomatoes, avocado, fried ginger, and chile; guacamole with pistachio salsa macha verde; tomato tostada with Robiola cheese, fried basil, and pickled red onions; scallop aguachile. OPPOSITE, FROM TOP: Fresh blue corn masa is rolled into thin sheets; Núñez (middle) and his team at Suerte.

with Mexican ingredients like hibiscus and avocado, but also white soy, kombu, and black sesame seeds—all of which nod to his time in the kitchen at Uchiko, chef Tyson Cole's Japanese-inspired Austin institution.

Núñez, who was raised in the northern Mexican town of Torreón, figured out pretty quickly that he was meant to be in the kitchen. He spent a year in college in San Antonio, when he happened upon Anthony Bourdain's influential book, *Kitchen Confidential*. The book convinced him that cooking could be a career—though Núñez is quick to point out that he is drawn to the work and not to the partying culture Bourdain's book glorified.

At the age of 19, Núñez entered culinary school. He found that tasks like making the perfect broth and deboning chickens came naturally to him. Though he did not miss being at a traditional university, he was envious of his friends' spring break trips, so he planned one of his own, to Europe, sleeping on the couch in a friend's living room in San Antonio to save up money. The experience opened Núñez's mind to what food could be—and quickly humbled him. "I thought I was God's gift to cooking, but I quickly realized that when you go to Italy, you would see people in hostels that are making pasta better than any restaurant in the U.S.," he says with a laugh.

Núñez returned to Texas, where he worked at celebrated Austin restaurant La Condesa and staged at Barley Swine, eventually becoming the chef de cuisine at Launderette. He was making plans to cook in New York when his now-business partner Sam Hellman-Mass approached him about opening Núñez's dream restaurant, one centered on masa. "Mexican food, to me, was always something that I was passionate about because it meant something to me, and a tortilla—it's the canvas of Mexican cooking," he says. "I was immediately passionate about the concept."

Núñez, who had just turned 28, initially felt like he might be too young to run such a project, but he gave himself until the age of 30 for it to work out. "I've always been of the mindset that if I'm going to gamble on something, it might as well be on myself," he says. Safe to say, the gamble has paid off. Núñez recently celebrated his 33rd birthday, and Suerte is busier than ever with Núñez spreading the gospel of good tortillas to everyone who walks through the doors.

FERMÍN'S AUSTIN CITY GUIDE

DESTINATION BARBECUE

"There are so many people who are doing barbecue great, such as Franklin Barbecue, Kerlin BBQ, Distant Relatives, and La Barbecue. But I think the person that truly takes traditional barbecue and flips it on its head, with the respect it deserves, showcasing the city for who we are, is Evan LeRoy of **LeRoy and Lewis Barbecue** *(leroyandlewisbbq .com)*. LeRoy's way of cooking new-school barbecue shows the talent we have in Austin. He knows the rules, and he knows how much he can bend them."

BEST BREAKFAST

"The carne guisada at **Joe's Bakery** *(joes bakery.com)* is the best way to start any morning, but especially Sunday mornings, because that's usually the start of my weekend. Their flour tortillas always remind me of the ones I ate while growing up in northern Mexico."

WINE & DINE

"Beverage director Alex Bell at **Aviary Wine & Kitchen** *(aviarywine kitchen.com)* describes wine with such grace and approachability, you know anything he offers is something he would want to drink himself. Chef Andre Molina speaks the same language in the kitchen.

The food and wine complement each other in a way that every wine bar should strive for."

DAY DRINKS

"At **Kalimotxo** *(kalimotxoatx.com)*, I always start with the Café de Noche, which reminds me of a carajillo, with vodka, coffee, toasted bran caramel, and chocolate mole bitters. It sounds like a lot but is extremely balanced and a great pick-me-up. Another must is the Clear As Day, with mezcal, Dolin Blanc, Falernum, and orange bitters. It's a clear drink that looks like water and is the perfect refreshing beverage. I wish I had it on tap at my house! All of the cocktails are world-class and extremely crushable, elaborate without being intimidating."

SECRET SPOTS

"The tacos at **Cuantos Tacos** *(on Instagram @cuantostacos512)* taste like some of my favorite taquerias in Mexico City, which are hard to find on this side of the border. **Nixta Taqueria** *(nixta taqueria.com)* takes the taco and gives it back through the eyes of a chef; Edgar Rico knows what he's doing, and I'm here for it. **Bad Larry Burger Club** *(on Instagram @badlarry burgerclub)* makes the type of burgers I want to eat after a long day in the kitchen."

Angel Barreto

ANJU, WASHINGTON, D.C.

A LIFELONG STUDENT OF KOREAN FOOD, THIS BEST NEW CHEF WANTS TO EDUCATE AND INFORM DINERS ABOUT THE CUISINE, WITH A BOUNDARY-PUSHING MENU THAT LOOKS BOTH TO THE PAST AND TO THE FUTURE FOR INSPIRATION.

PHOTOGRAPHY BY ALEX LAU

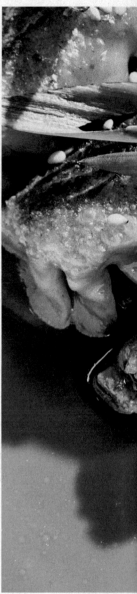

hanging out in Korean barbecue spots until 3 or 4 a.m. "I love the freshness, the crunchiness, the funkiness of it," he explains. He bristles at the idea that it's strange for him to be cooking Korean food. "Your diaspora does not dictate what you can do in life."

If someone had any lingering doubt about Barreto's grasp on Korean cuisine, it would melt away the instant an order of fried chicken arrived at the table at Anju. There has been no dearth of excellent Korean fried chicken around the country in recent years, but Barreto's is somehow both crispier and lighter than the rest. He brines the meat with Korean long peppers, garlic, onions, salt, and sugar and dredges it twice to create the shatteringly crisp skin. It's then fried twice, tossed in a sticky gochujang glaze, and drizzled with Alabama-style white barbecue sauce. "The sauce cuts through the sweetness and spiciness," he says.

Before he started his career in restaurants, Barreto had planned to study international relations, but he found he hated it in practice during an externship. After learning that a friend had enrolled in culinary school, Barreto followed suit, attending L'Academie de Cuisine in Gaithersburg, Maryland. Although he studied French food, he gravitated toward Asian flavors and landed a spot at The Source, Wolfgang Puck's

WHEN ANGEL BARRETO WAS FIRST SETTING UP the accounts with suppliers for Anju, the restaurant he helms in Washington, D.C., a salesperson didn't believe he was serious when he ordered 150 pounds of salted shrimp. Even though the store had it in stock, the salesperson said he didn't think that Barreto actually "needed" the ingredient. It's not the first time someone was surprised that Barreto, who is half Puerto Rican and half Black, runs one of D.C.'s most popular Korean restaurants. "There's very few [chefs] who look like me that cook Asian food," he says, with more empathy than frustration in his voice.

Korean flavors were a part of Barreto's childhood. Both of his parents lived in Korea while serving in the military; his mother, a formidable cook, would re-create Korean dishes at home. "She loved the flavors, the dynamism of the people," he explains. "She loved everything." As a young cook, Barreto also found himself drawn to the cuisine, often

ANGEL'S D.C.
CITY GUIDE

A STORIED SMOKE

"The half-smoke is the most quintessential D.C. dish. It's a smoked sausage made with half beef and half pork, served with onions, mustard, or chili. The best version is from **Ben's Chili Bowl** (*bens chilibowl.com*), where civil rights leaders and celebrities have flocked for 62 years." (See "The Matriarch" on p. 168 for more about Ben's.)

SHOP & NOSH

"**FreshFarm Market** (*freshfarm.org*) in Dupont is an eight-minute walk from Anju. It's open on the weekend, and there's a fantastic variety of local produce, meats, cheese, and flowers. Some of my favorite vendors are **Seylou Bakery** for fresh-milled flour, bread, and pastries, and **Puddin'** for chicken and beef sausage gumbo and brown butter bourbon pudding."

BEST BRUNCH

"Chef Matt Conroy of **Lutèce** (*lutecedc.com*) is whipping up food that's fun yet rooted in French-inspired technique and flavor, like avocado tartine with mushroom hash and pain perdu with cherries and almonds."

RUM LOVERS, REJOICE

"**Cotton & Reed** (*cottonandreed.com*), tucked in Union Market, is a rum bar that exceeds expectations. They only offer rum, no wine or beer. My favorite cocktail is the Liquid Nostalgia, a blend of white rum, blood orange, and Rujero Singani [a Bolivian grape spirit] that tastes like an orange creamsicle."

PIES THAT SURPRISE

"All-Purpose Pizzeria (*allpurposedc.com*) does a Jersey-style pizza called Enzo the Baker with Bianco DiNapoli tomatoes, Calabro mozzarella, capicola bacon, spicy chiles, pickled peppers, and basil. These flavors work so well with their chewy crust."

SOUVENIR ALERT

"Angel Gregorio's love of spices and travel is evident at her shop, **The Spice Suite** (*thespice suite.com*), where she offers some of the most creative blends of oils and spices you can find. Each month, Gregorio sells "SpiceBoxes" that contain unique, curated products and sell out within minutes."

CHEF'S NIGHT OUT

"Chef Damian Brown of **The Uncaged Chefs** (*theuncagedchefs .com*) has no rules. His dishes, like jerk brisket tacos and peach cobbler chicken and waffles, have big flavor and bigger impact. Brown is always whipping up something new and crazy, like Fruity Pebbles cinnamon buns with cereal milk icing."

now-shuttered pan-Asian behemoth, where in about six years he became executive sous chef. During this time, he met chef Danny Lee, who approached him to run Anju.

At Anju (which means "drinking food"), Barreto serves modern dishes like honey-lacquered sweet potatoes with a mound of fluffy sesame whipped cream straight from an iSi canister, and a tender, salty kimchi potato pancake paired with plenty of crème fraîche. But all of it is rooted in tradition. "It always has to be based in Korean food and society," Barreto explains. While innovating, he also brings older techniques and recipes to the menu, like a snappy and gently bitter banchan made from bellflower root.

Barreto is a practicing Buddhist, which informs his approach to leadership in the kitchen. "One of the things that's healthy to learn is slowing down," he says. "We always say we're in the hospitality industry, but sometimes that hospitality doesn't extend to our workers. I wish going forward that we extend it—not only to our guests, but also to our staff members."

OPPOSITE: Sticky-sweet Korean fried chicken with Alabama-style white barbecue sauce. ABOVE: Barreto's mandu (with a filling of pork and kimchi) are pan-fried, served in a pool of soy sauce, and topped with scallions and sesame seeds.

Ji Hye Kim

MISS KIM, ANN ARBOR, MICHIGAN

INSPIRED BY MICHIGAN INGREDIENTS AND MEMORIES OF HER MOTHER'S COOKING, THIS BEST NEW CHEF OFFERS LESSONS IN THE HISTORY OF KOREAN CUISINE INTERSPERSED AMONG LAYERS OF FLAVOR AND TEXTURE.

PHOTOGRAPHY BY CEDRIC ANGELES

JI HYE'S ANN ARBOR CITY GUIDE

"A LOT OF PEOPLE have known since the age of 3 that they want to be a chef," says Ji Hye Kim, who owns Miss Kim in Ann Arbor, Michigan. "That's not my story at all. I was 30 when I started thinking about it." Kim grew up in Seoul, South Korea. Her mom was a talented cook, so in many ways Kim, now 43, took good food for granted. "It has always been there in my life." But Kim's mom would never let her help in the kitchen, and at a certain point, Kim stopped trying.

Kim's family emigrated from South Korea to New Jersey when she was 13, and she eventually moved to Ann Arbor to attend the University of Michigan. After graduating, she worked in accounts receivable at a hospital. (Today, Kim likes to joke that she went from "hospital to hospitality.") On a whim, she applied for a job at Zingerman's Delicatessen. It entailed a 90% pay cut, but she fell in love with the work. Through a program at Zingerman's, she put herself through "culinary business school," working in the delicatessen kitchen and on the line at Roadhouse, Zingerman's full-service restaurant. At the same time, she started running a food truck, laying the groundwork for her restaurant, Miss Kim, which opened in 2016.

For Miss Kim, Kim went into "nerd mode" researching Korean cuisine using historical cookbooks. "I wasn't interested in what's being done now, or even what was done 50 years ago," she explains. "I wanted to look back a few centuries." She also wanted to tap into the food she was raised on, where her mother made everything from scratch, and to emphasize local Michigan produce. For the tteokbokki on her menu–informed by a recipe once served at the royal palace in Seoul–batons of chewy rice cakes are crisped and tossed in a sweet and savory sauce with shiitake mushrooms, seasonal vegetables, and a poached egg. Where most Korean restaurants in America serve a standardized bibimbap, Kim showcases regional differences. She's served a North Korean version, tossing the rice with pork fat and topping it with thick slices of pork belly and toasted seaweed. She looked to mountain communities for a bibimbap where rice and potato form a crust at the bottom of the bowl. Another version, inspired by the eating habits of Korean monks (who avoid alliums and only eat what is available within a certain distance of their temple), featured local vegetables, multigrain rice, and a soy vinaigrette.

She usually has a calm demeanor, but there are few things that frustrate Kim more than the expectation that her food should be "cheap." Those expectations are not placed on a nearby Italian restaurant that charges $22 for five pieces of ravioli, she points out. Factor in that Kim buys exclusively from local farms, pays her staff fairly, and offers health insurance, scholarships, and massage credits, and the prices (entrées range from $14–$24 per dish) feel correct.

It may have taken Kim a long time to realize this was where she wanted to be, but she plans to stay. She hopes to collect the historical recipes she loves in a cookbook and wants to open a smaller operation that focuses on the plant-based cooking of Korean Buddhists. In many ways, Kim now sees cooking as her mission: "I'm just playing a small role in the work of how food evolves and how people live."

FROM TOP: Three takes on bibimbap at Miss Kim, all served in stone bowls: North Korean–inspired bibimbap with pork belly, cucumber banchan, bean sprout banchan, greens, toasted nori, and edible flowers over rice; Jeonju bibimbap with beef tartare, banchan, squash blossoms, and a soft egg; and a potato-and-rice bibimbap topped with pickled onions and scallions

THE CITY SIGNATURE
"If there's only one place you can visit in Ann Arbor, go to **Zingerman's** (zinger mans.com). Order the Reuben—the '#2,' as the regulars call it, or 'a killer,' in President Obama's words. It's simple but classic: a huge sandwich made with slices of Jewish rye bread from Zingerman's Bakehouse, local corned beef from United Meat and Deli, sauerkraut from The Brinery, Swiss cheese, and homemade Russian dressing."

THE DRINKUBATOR
"**The Bar at 327 Braun Court** (brauncourt .com) is located in an unassuming house in a courtyard of shops. The cocktails are so good; it's the only place in the world where I'd happily order a White Russian, made with fresh heavy cream from the local Calder Dairy. The Bar has been hosting small food entrepreneurs for years, and many have spun out to open their own restaurants. (I was one of them, and so was Spencer, another local favorite.) The current residency is **Prismo's**, which specializes in Neapolitan-style pizza made with naturally leavened pizza dough and locally sourced seasonal ingredients."

BRUNCH ON THE GO
"On Saturday mornings, I love walking around the **Ann Arbor Farmers Market** and grabbing croissants and butter from **White Lotus Farms** (whitelotusfarms .com), radishes from **Goetz Greenhouse,** pita and spreads from **HumusFalafel,** and a baguette from **Café Japon** (cafejapon.net), where they pair Asian flavors with French techniques and make my favorite pastries, like apricot danishes and red bean buns. Ann Arbor has 161 parks, so I'd walk to one in the area, like **Wheeler Park** (named after the city's first African American mayor) for a picnic. I'd also bring a bottle from **Ground Control Wines** (groundcontrolwines .com) because 11 a.m. on a weekend is a perfect time for a glass."

CHEF'S NIGHT OUT
"The menu at **Spencer** (spencerannarbor.com) changes often, and the food is delicious and complex. It's a treasured neighborhood restaurant with casual but friendly service. It's where I'd choose to go for a rare night off."

MICHIGAN MEAD
"**Bløm Meadworks** (drinkblom.com) makes session meads and ciders that are pleasantly bubbly and not too sweet, all from Michigan ingredients. While you can find their meads and ciders elsewhere, I prefer to drink their rotating seasonal flavors on their patio."

Blake Aguillard & Trey Smith

SAINT-GERMAIN,
NEW ORLEANS

IN A FORMER PIZZA JOINT IN THE BYWATER NEIGHBORHOOD, THE CHEFS
AND CO-OWNERS OF SAINT-GERMAIN ARE SERVING THE MOST CREATIVE,
AMBITIOUS, AND ACCESSIBLE TASTING MENU IN THE NATION.

PHOTOGRAPHY BY CEDRIC ANGELES

"BLAKE [AGUILLARD] AND I VIEW CUISINE somewhere between a sport and an art," says Trey Smith. "We like to push things as far as we can." The chefs and co-owners of Saint-Germain in New Orleans are always drying, curing, or fermenting something at their restaurant. A batch of local tomatoes dries in the sun on the balcony of the tin roof, after which they will ferment for a month. Scraps of venison become garum, a fish sauce–like condiment that takes three months to make. They once created a vegan cheese course by preserving turnips and then washing them with the culture they use to make cheeses. "When you would eat these turnips, they tasted like Brie," Smith rhapsodizes.

The two chefs met as young line cooks, working their way up the ladder at Restaurant August under the guidance of the chef de cuisine at the time, Michael Gulotta. Aguillard and Smith bonded immediately: "We both took every level of cooking very seriously," says Smith.

Their backgrounds couldn't be more different. A Louisiana native, Aguillard wanted to be a chef from a young age and is dedicated to the technical aspects of cooking. At one point, he even left the chef de cuisine position at Gulotta's restaurant MoPho, which he had helped open, to work as a line cook at Saison in San Francisco. "I just wanted to do more learning," says Aguillard. Smith, on the other hand, spent his childhood visiting New Mexico and pursued an economics degree, followed by law school, before realizing that he wanted to cook. While Aguillard was at Saison, Smith stayed in New Orleans, helping Gulotta open Maypop and getting "really involved on the business side."

When Aguillard returned to New Orleans, it became clear that between his expertise and Smith's business acumen, it was time to open a restaurant. With Drew Delaughter, Saint-Germain's third partner who oversees front-of-house operations (who Smith met while attending the Culinary Institute of America in Hyde Park, New York, and who also worked as the general manager at MoPho), Aguillard and Smith opened Saint-Germain in 2018 in a former pizza place in the Bywater neighborhood.

Saint-Germain is one of just a handful of restaurants in New Orleans to offer a tasting menu, and it's one of the most exciting, and affordable, in the nation. (In April, my five-course tasting menu was $79, plus tax and tip.)

The Saint-Germain Table Salad (AT RIGHT) includes seasonal vegetable crudités sprinkled with crispy wild rice and tarragon buttermilk for dunking. The Levain Cornbread (OPPOSITE) is served with black carrot salt and cultured butter that has been aged up to two and a half years. It is shown here with cantaloupe, spruce, and Ibérico ham.

The reservation-only 12-seat dining room is an intimate affair, where nightly changing dishes like a small brick of toasted sourdough soaked in a sauce of chicken jus, sherry, and Roquefort cheese and blanketed with a dry-aged beef tartare are placed in front of you. No reservations are required for the wine bar, where seating spills into the dreamy backyard, and it's easy to pass several hours with heavy pours of natural wines and the crudité platter, which on my visit included daikon compressed in sweet soy sauce and a shower of crispy wild rice.

The two chefs hope that Saint-Germain can be a blueprint for others. They have no desire to add more seats, even if it means passing up the opportunity to make more money. Expanding capacity would mean compromising on how they love to cook. "With our hyper-focused model, you don't need 200 people to understand what you're doing," says Smith. "You only need 15 to 20 people per night who get you."

LIKE A LOCAL

BLAKE & TREY'S
NOLA CITY GUIDE

WORTH THE WAIT
TREY: "When I think about a dish that people in New Orleans go out for, the po'boy comes to mind. My personal favorite is the shrimp po'boy from **Guy's Po-boys** (facebook.com/guyspoboysnola). It's a small shop that's always busy but definitely worth the wait." **BLAKE:** "I don't know anyone that can make beignets at home as good as **Café Du Monde** (cafedumonde.com). Their beignets are the perfect way to start off a quintessential New Orleans day."

COCKTAIL CITY

TREY: "My favorite cocktail is an old-fashioned, and **Cure** (*curenola .com*) knows how to bring it to life."

BLAKE: "The whiskey milk punch from **Bar Tonique** (*bartonique .com*) is my favorite cocktail in the city."

PASSION-FUELED PASTRY

BLAKE: "I love the cinnamon roll from **Levee Baking Company** (*leveebakingco.com*). They sprinkle them with sugar, and the dough is light and airy."

TREY: "I had a Parker House roll stuffed with pimiento cheese at **Molly's Rise and Shine** (*mollysriseandshine .com*), and it still lives on in my mind. The team there has such passion; it comes through in the food and service, and it's one of my favorite spots for pastries (and everything else)."

EDIBLE GIFTS

TREY: "I love to buy gifts at **Bellegarde Bakery** (*bellegardebakery .com*). They carefully source and grind their flours, cornmeal, and grits. A bag of fresh-ground flour or cornmeal with a recipe is always a fun gift."

LOCAL HEROES

BLAKE: "Melissa Martin at **Mosquito Supper Club** (*mosquitosupper club.com*) is doing small-batch Louisiana dishes in an intimate setting. At **Dakar Nola** (*on Instagram @dakar nola*), Senegalese chef Serigne Mbaye has been doing a pop-up. He's one of the most driven cooks I've met."

TREY: "High Hat (*high hatcafe.com*) is a no-fuss Southern spot that always delivers. Co-owner Adolfo Garcia is a great example of someone who really supports other restaurants."

Gaby Maeda

STATE BIRD PROVISIONS,
SAN FRANCISCO

KINDNESS IN THE KITCHEN IS AS IMPORTANT AS CREATIVITY TO THIS CHEF, WHO
DRAWS ON THE FLAVORS OF HER HONOLULU CHILDHOOD TO CREATE A MENU THAT'S
PART HAWAIIAN, PART CALIFORNIAN, AND ENTIRELY HER OWN.

PHOTOGRAPHY BY AUBRIE PICK

"EVERY DAY WHEN I GO TO WORK, I am just as excited as I was on day one," declares Gaby Maeda. Maeda is the chef de cuisine at State Bird Provisions in San Francisco, where she and her team whip up a menu of punchy California cuisine, heavy on the local produce and with strong Asian influences. She has worked in professional kitchens for over a decade and a half, and that is where she is happiest.

Maeda was drawn to restaurant work as a teen in Honolulu but has never been in a rush to make it to the top of the ladder. She has always been more interested in gaining skills than accolades (though she has received those, too, including a James Beard nomination). At 14, she convinced her parents to let her homeschool herself, with two conditions: that she get good grades and a job. Maeda started working as a cashier at a Japanese delicatessen, but she wished she were cooking. "I wanted to be where the action was," she recalls. When she turned 16, she landed her first back-of-house job. She didn't know what she was doing half the time, so she got a textbook from the Culinary Institute of America and practiced how to braise, chiffonade, and brunoise at home. Setting her sights on San Francisco, she moved to the mainland to attend culinary school, which led to an externship at Gary Danko. She ended up staying for five years, mastering each and every station, leaving with the title of lead line cook. "I never became a sous chef, and I was totally fine with that," she says. "I was proud of what I learned and for being treated with respect as an out, gay, young kid."

At 24, Maeda started cooking at State Bird Provisions and instantly connected with chef and co-owner Stuart Brioza (a 2003 F&W Best New Chef). "He had a plan for me before I had a plan for me," she says. Maeda was quickly promoted to sous chef, and just over a year later, she was offered the chef de cuisine job. Maeda felt comfortable in her cooking skills, but it was important to her to learn how to become a good manager, not wanting to repeat the yelling she had seen in other kitchens. "I wanted to make sure I knew how to schedule, how to deal with the stresses of everything," she says.

When she stepped into the role of chef de cuisine, she also found her culinary point of view–one grounded in, but not bound by, her past. "Hawaii is such a melting pot," says Maeda. "You grow up cooking and eating Korean food, Chinese food, and Filipino food, even if you are not from these cultures." Those influences are a through line at State Bird Provisions. A dish of carrot mochi uses the chewy pounded rice in a gnocchi-like preparation. It's part of a dish where Maeda cooks carrots in three additional ways: roasted, pickled, and juiced in a supple vinaigrette. Another childhood treat is the inspiration for a dish of egg tofu (made by steaming eggs, dashi, white soy, and mirin), cubed and crowned with pickled mushrooms and housemade chile oil. And then there is the riff on shrimp toast, where slices of milk bread are topped with shrimp poached with lemongrass, galangal, and lime leaf and then tossed in a curry oil aioli and showered with celery and cilantro.

One day, Maeda, now 31, wants her own spot, but she's in no rush. "I would hope that in 10 years, I would open my own restaurant," she says. "I will only do it if I can do it right."

Maeda's corn mochi (made in-house using mochiko flour from nearby Koda Farms) is seared in butter and finished with charred corn husk powder. It sits on corn puree that's seasoned with lime zest and juice, and it gets smothered with grilled corn planks, goat's milk Gouda, lime-pickled Fresno chiles, cilantro, and basil and dusted with pickled chile powder.

THE SF SIGNATURE

"Anytime a friend, family member, or new cook comes to the city, the first thing I tell them to do is to get a burrito in the Mission District. **El Farolito** (*elfarolitosf .com*) is a well-loved taqueria in the Mission, and their burritos, suizas, and salsas are delicious. I go there for the Super Suiza (quesadilla with carne asada, avocado, and sour cream) and smother it with salsa verde and pickled jalapeños."

THIS IS THE PLACE

"The place I would take an out-of-town friend for cocktails in the Bay Area is **Friends and Family** (*friendsand familybar.com*) in Oakland. It's a woman-owned, queer-owned business that opened during the pandemic. It was a place I was very excited to check out, and when I finally did, it was everything I hoped it would be. The drinks are outstanding; the vibe is fun, quirky, and chill; and the food matches well."

LOCAL HAUNT

"**Birba** (*birbawine .com*) is a wine bar in Hayes Valley where the wine list is eclectic, and I always end up drinking something that I've never heard of and start loving from that moment on. They have a great back patio, and I usually enjoy their pistachio-feta dip with ice-cold crudités, as well as their tinned fish with marinated white beans, lemon, and crackers. It's my favorite place to hang out on a day off. On Sundays, Birba is home to an amazing Thai pop-up called Intu-On."

CARBS FOREVER

"**Del Popolo** (*delpopolo sf.com*) has been my favorite pizza for a few years. I love the chewy texture of the dough and the sourness from it being naturally fermented. They opened their brick-and-mortar in an old acting studio on Bush Street that I used to walk past every day on my way to work. My favorite is the potato pizza with fontina and rosemary. I love a good carb-on-carb dish!"

NEIGHBORHOOD VIBE

"My favorite restaurant in the city right now is **Pearl 6101** (*pearl6101 .com*). It's a neighborhood spot in Outer Richmond, and they have such a beautiful space. Chef-owner Mel Lopez is very talented, and I crave the dishes she cooks. It's a place I want to take my family."

BAKERS GONNA BAKE

"**Josey Baker Bread** (*joseybakerbread .com*) grinds their flour in-house and has an amazing presence in the Bay Area restaurant community. We use their buckwheat flour, red wheat flour, cornmeal, and whole-grain mix in our own recipes at State Bird."

Lucas Sin

NICE DAY AND JUNZI KITCHEN,
NEW YORK CITY

THROUGH A DELICIOUS DEEP DIVE INTO RESEARCH AND DEVELOPMENT
AND A VISIONARY NEW BUSINESS MODEL, THIS BEST NEW CHEF
WANTS TO CHANGE THE WAY YOU THINK ABOUT AMERICAN CHINESE FOOD.

PHOTOGRAPHY BY ALEX LAU

LUCAS SIN IS ON A MISSION to perfect General Tso's chicken. His goal: to make a version of the dish for Nice Day, his modern American Chinese restaurant in New York, that retains its crispness, with a sauce that's viscous but not gloopy, garlicky but not too hot.

General Tso's is one of the most popular items at American Chinese restaurants, and yet, according to Sin's research, there is no standard way to make it. He has combed through cookbooks, spent hours scouring the internet, tasted as many versions as he could track down, and spoken with chefs around the country, but no one can agree on what makes General Tso's so distinctively delicious. Some say the key ingredient is honey; others swear by the addition of ketchup; one chef is certain that the sauce needs brown sugar. Sin's solution? Combine them all. Sin also omits cornstarch and water from his recipe. "Adding water will just make it soggy as it is being delivered," says Sin. He is correct. The version that arrived at my hotel door had just begun to slide into that blissful textural point of crispy-gone-soggy—emphasis on lingering crispy. Mission accomplished.

Sin grew up in Hong Kong. As a middle schooler, he went to summer camp in the United States, which is where he was introduced to American Chinese food. Every Tuesday night like clockwork, he remembers, a Honda would pull up to the camp dorms. The driver would pop the trunk to reveal containers of fried rice, General Tso's chicken, and sesame chicken. "The first thing I realized was I cannot tell the difference between orange chicken and sesame chicken and General Tso's chicken," Sin says with a laugh. "But it was delicious." It also left an impression.

LUCAS' NYC CITY GUIDE

PIZZA TOWN
"The NYC dollar slice is a dying breed, and **Percy's Pizza** (percyspizza.com) on Bleecker Street serves the best one. The bottom is crispy like a cracker, the low-moisture mozzarella is abundant, and the tomato sauce is flavorful. In the economic downturn of the pandemic, Percy's went through the effort to redesign their logo and awning to replace the '$1' sign with a '$2' sign. It's a two-dollar slice now, but still worth every penny."

Cooking became a long-term side hustle for Sin. In high school, he ran a pop-up restaurant out of an abandoned factory in Hong Kong. After moving to New Haven, Connecticut, to attend Yale, the pop-ups continued in the basement of his dorm, where he cooked everything from zhuzhed-up instant noodles to five-course menus. "At some point, we were doing 250 covers a weekend," says Sin. While other students chased internships, Sin spent his summers cooking in restaurants in Japan. While working for chef Yoshihiro Murata, the chef-owner of Kikunoi in Tokyo and Kyoto who is celebrated for preserving and innovating Japanese foodways, it struck Sin that he could bring Murata's approach to Chinese food.

When Sin returned to New Haven, his friends Yong Zhao and Wanting Zhang suggested opening a fast-casual Chinese restaurant called Junzi, combining Chinese culinary traditions—like Cantonese barbecue chicken and knife-cut noodles—in new, accessible formats. They opened locations in New Haven and New York City. During the pandemic, Sin converted the downtown Junzi location into a Nice Day outpost, where he re-engaged with the story of American Chinese food.

At Nice Day, Sin spends most of his time developing recipes, like sweet-and-sour sauce with traditional hawthorn berries, or sesame noodles that don't get soggy, as well as novel creations like a flaky egg roll wrapper stuffed with hamburger meat and cheese. A particular favorite of mine: Shake shake shrimp, a dish inspired by McDonald's, comes with a choice of sauce on the side—the diner combines the two when they are ready to eat, so the shrimp retains its crunch.

Sin may have a degree in cognitive science, but it's clear he is working on a PhD in global Chinese cooking. He can rattle off the history of chow mein, or break down the regional differences between American Chinese cooking in Michigan versus Seattle. He appears to think

THIS PAGE, CLOCKWISE FROM TOP: A dessert of peanut butter–and–coconut jam French toast with ice cream; yuzu slaw; cheeseburger egg rolls; General Tso's chicken; Impossible dan dan noodles; string beans; Seattle-style chicken teriyaki; sweet-and-sour pork belly; and crunchy cucumber salad OPPOSITE: Sin's General Tso's chicken sandwich

in Venn diagrams of how Chinese cooking techniques and flavors overlap and connect with other cuisines of the world.

Over the past few years, American Chinese restaurants have started to close at a rapid clip—a trend accelerated by the pandemic and the rise of anti-Asian racism. Sin is hopeful that Nice Day will honor and preserve these restaurants, not only literally, by taking over and converting them into Nice Day locations, in some cases, but also by increasing the appreciation of American Chinese food.

Nice Day will soon expand into a second location in Long Island. Sin has national aspirations but is building methodically, writing detailed training documents and creating a reliable supply chain. Sin wants to push American Chinese food toward sustainability in the broadest sense. "It needs to be sustainable when it comes to people: their mental health, their finances. That's the biggest thing."

CREATIVE CANTONESE
"**August Gatherings** (augustgatheringsny .com) serves the best Cantonese food in Manhattan; it's elegant and extraordinary. I go there when I need a spark of creativity. There are two dishes that blow me out of the water: wild octopus and bone marrow fusilli, a wok-fried take on Michelin-starred Marea's signature pasta, and the oven-roasted Angus short rib, which is slow-cooked in goose fat, flash-seared in a wok, and served with oyster sauce and broccoli."

COCKTAIL HOUR
"At **Double Chicken Please** (doublechicken please.com), I drink whatever bartenders GN Chan and Faye Chen hand me, like Negronis that take on hints of red bell pepper and shots accented with savory sour plum."

DIVINE DUMPLINGS
"**Shu Jiao Fu Zhou** (shujiaofuzhou.com) is a quaint corner dumpling restaurant that specializes in Fujianese peanut noodles, wontons, and pork-and-chive dumplings. It's unpretentious, honest, and quiet. No hullabaloo."

A NO-FUSS BURGER
"My favorite burger is at **Joe Junior** in Gramercy (167 Third Ave.). Always cooked to your liking, served by kind waiters, and no more than $7. It's so juicy, the bottom bun dissolves by the time you're halfway through."

MY DAILY SWEETS
"**Spongies** (121 Baxter St.) and **Kam Hing** (118 Baxter St.) serve the airiest sponge cakes for 85 cents. I pair them with yuenyeung, which is half coffee, half milk tea. And **Kamboat** (111 Bowery) makes the best egg tarts in town."

The Matriarch

"Love each other. It's not that hard to do." *–VIRGINIA ALI*

THE BANQUETTES at Ben's Chili Bowl were packed. The stools were occupied. It was hard to get a seat at this D.C. institution, but the food came out quickly, so you only had to wait a few minutes for the tables to turn. It was 1963, and a young man waiting inside the restaurant was impatient and stressed. Virginia Ali, the proprietor of this local joint, could feel the man's angst and quickly cleared a table. "What's wrong?" she asked. "I've got this idea," he responded. "I just don't know how to execute it." Ali said, "Well, tell me what it is; maybe I can help." And the man said, "It's called the March on Washington." That man was, of course, Martin Luther King Jr., one of many influential Americans who dined regularly at the Chili Bowl, his heart fueled by Ali's famous half-smokes—a half beef, half pork sausage that's grilled, sandwiched in a steamed bun, and topped with mustard, onions, and housemade chili sauce. Ever since Ali and her late husband, Ben, opened the restaurant in 1958, a year after they met, the Chili Bowl has been a gathering place for people of all kinds, from community organizers to world leaders. In fact, when asked about her greatest achievement, Ali credits her ability to bring people together through food. That's exactly what she has done for 63 years, whipping up chili-cheese half-smokes for the masses and feeding the fight for racial equality. *–KWAME ONWUACHI,* FOOD & WINE *EXECUTIVE PRODUCER AND* TOP CHEF *JUDGE*

BY THE NUMBERS

$5,000
The amount of money Ben and Virginia Ali started with when they began renovating the building that would become Ben's Chili Bowl

7
Locations of Ben's Chili Bowl that exist today, including outposts at stadiums and airports

25M+
Half-smokes sold since the Chili Bowl opened in 1958

2M+
Gallons of chili sold at the Chili Bowl throughout the years

NO. 1
Seller: the half-smoke

2009
The year that President Barack Obama first dined at the Chili Bowl; it was January 10, and the meal was his first public outing as president-elect.

LIVING LEGEND

In August 2021, at the first-ever F&W Family Reunion—an event that celebrated diversity within the hospitality industry—Ali was given the Lifetime Achievement Award in recognition of her rich and vital contributions to both the D.C. community and the world at large.

Ludo Lefebvre

A Moment with the Master

Lexus Culinary Master Chef Ludo Lefebvre chats about his French roots, his pandemic pivots, and opening his first restaurant outside of L.A.

MICHELIN STARS, RAVE REVIEWS, A LEXUS CULINARY MASTER TITLE, and even a French knighthood—Ludo Lefebvre has earned them all. Raised in France, Lefebvre has built a mini-empire in Los Angeles, with various concepts that each draw upon his French training—then take those skills to new places. "As I always say, if you learn the basics and fundamentals first, you will have more freedom to take risks," notes the chef.

First came Trois Mec, which opened in 2013 and soon became the hottest ticket in town thanks to its cutting-edge tasting menus. Sadly, Lefebvre lost this Michelin-starred favorite during the pandemic, as "there was just no way to make the business model work," he reveals. Luckily, he still has other projects to helm, including Petit Trois, his classic French bistro, and Ludo Bird, his fast-casual ode to fried chicken.

This year is also full of other exciting things, including the opening of his first restaurant outside of L.A., and his appearance at the *Food & Wine* Classic in Aspen in September. Here, we chat with the master chef about the challenges of the past year, his plans for the future, and how food helped him fall in love with L.A.

Q+A

You have based your career in Los Angeles— what is it about L.A. that you love so much?

I didn't know what to expect when I moved here—I didn't speak English and I came with $200—but very quickly, I fell in love with the city and all it had to offer. I had never had things like sushi, Chinese food, tacos, and "American" hamburgers, so it was fun to explore all these foods and flavors. I think my love for the city was reflected in food. Every day is full of inspiration and I try to give back to the city the same passion it gives me.

What were some ways you were able to work with your community during the lockdown, when the restaurants were closed?

For the first few months, we assisted Chef

FOOD & WINE.

THE RESTAURANT ISSUE

↘ MEET AMERICA'S BEST NEW CHEFS P. 125

9 FOOD CITIES TO VISIT NOW
P. 131

THE NEW RULES OF DINING OUT
P. 46

OCTOBER 2021

B Hereford Branch
October, 2021

SWEET POTATO STICKY
BUNS WITH TOASTED
MARSHMALLOW FROM
L.A.'S ALL DAY BABY P. 142